Composting the Ego

Leaf Lessons II

Composting the Ego

Angie Harris

Leaf Lessons II

Composting the Ego

©Copyright @ 2023 Angela Marie Harris

To request permission, contact publisher at

www.leaflessons.org

ISBN: 979-8-9862705-5-5

Edited by: Clelia Lewis

Cover by: buckely_studlo

Photo: Angela Harris

Reference World English Bible; The World English Bible (WEB) is a Public Domain (no copyright) Modern English translation of the Holy Bible. That means that you may freely copy it in any form, including electronic and print formats. The World English Bible is based on the American Standard Version of the Holy Bible first published in 1901, the Biblia Hebraica Stutgartensa Old Testament, and the Greek Majority Text New Testament. It is in draft form, and currently being edited for accuracy and readability.

Acknowledgements & Dedication

I cannot say there is a particular person that inspired this book. In many ways, life itself has been my teacher, and the many lessons it has taught me created these pages. But there are also individuals who have challenged me, pushing me towards living as my highest self, and had I not had these people in my life, I never would have overcome the many insecurities held in my body that kept me imprisoned to my past. Taking the leap of continuing the *Leaf Lessons* series and writing *Composting the Ego* is a direct response to all of this generous help and guidance.

In recent years, the healing that has taken place in my life has opened me up to opportunities I never could have imagined. Becoming more aligned with my highest self, finding my life-purpose, and working towards building my dreams once only seemed a fairytale, a vision I would never accomplish. The key has been learning to truly love myself as I am.

It's never easy to even look at, let alone expose areas of your life that have caused deep pain or debilitating shame. But because I was able to find support that allowed me to feel seen, heard, and valued, I began to be able to see, hear, and value myself. This naturally leads to change, and I have and continue to become a better version of myself—not by rejecting but by fulling accepting myself in my wholeness.

Throughout the healing process, listening to and aligning myself with my highest self, the many walls that keep me from living AS my true self slowly fall away. I call this "composting" my own ego. My gratitude for the support I've received in reaching the place I have is immeasurable. Joe, without your help in getting through the inner conflicts and turmoil the first book brought up for me, this one would not exist. So, for that reason *Composting the Ego* has been dedicated to you. Thank you!

Table of Contents:

Preface

Finding the right words to describe what this book holds within its pages is a challenge. The insights we gain about our ego's many challenges and the obstacles we face as we strive to live the life we truly desire, are themselves providing intuitive guidance and support. Contrary to what many may think, it is essential to befriend our egos. Through acceptance, our ego becomes an important part of what guides us towards connecting with our highest self. From mental to physical health, our ego plays an important role in our human experience. *Composting the Ego* teaches us how the obstacles we overcome are also important in the process of enhancing our lives and connecting with our spirit.

While writing this book, I found myself continually evaluating what was being written in the pages, paying attention to my own ego's programming, to avoid creating more barriers to my highest self and to guiding others to connect to theirs. Of course the words you find will include a bit of my ego as well as my spirit's intuitive insights, as we cannot fully separate the two in this human life. However, upon reflection and to my best ability, when I noticed my words fully immersed in my ego, I took the time to observe and adjust and rewrite them from a freer place. Many times I found myself rewriting entire chapters, or completely erasing them all together and starting over. This book challenged me to increase my capacity to compost the lessons of my ego and to let go and trust my spirit, developing a deeper connection with my intuition. Growth is a lifelong journey, and I am aware that I will always be in a process of unlearning and relearning. My desire is to always work towards expanding my understanding of the spirit and connect deeper with my highest self.

I hope this book helps you to do the same and to release old programming that has kept you in cycles you wish to let go. I also hope it helps you develop a deeper love for yourself and grace for the journey of self-development and growth.

Some of the things you read in this book may be triggering to the ego, possibly even cause you to question things as you have known them to be, or even causing a feeling of disagreement, fear or anger to arise within. I invite you to allow all these emotions to surface and to evaluate each one. This is part of allowing the book's message to stir things up, which is also part of composting the ego.

You will see some repeated messages throughout the book, and I encourage you to remain in an energy of trusting the flow as it was written, and the intuitive insights it brings. I believe the Universe purposely repeated many of the lessons in this book to help us fully grasp what it was trying to teach us.

If you have chosen this book based on the title, it is very likely that you are seeking some sort of healing, growth, or development of self, to connect deeper with your highest self. I hope you can find what you are seeking in these pages, even if it is simply a review of things already known. Take what resonates with your spirit and leave the parts that do not. It is not my desire to convince you to believe, think the same, or even behave as I do. It is simply my desire to encourage, support, and challenge you to be fully yourself, connected to who you are meant to be in this lifetime; to help you reflect on things you have known to be true, and maybe even expand yourself beyond the known into something new.

I fully trust that your spirit will guide you and connect you with your highest self as you seek to expand, learn, and grow. We are all on our own individual journeys, even as we are linked by universal truth and ebullient love, and because of that, I trust you will find compassion in the words of this book as you wade into the journey of Composting the Ego.

Chapter 1

"I am"

The ego gets a bad rap in spiritual communities.
Much like programming in a religious setting,
you may find yourself falling into accepted
patterns of thinking in spiritual communities.
Labels such as *New Age*, *Lightworker*, *Star
Seed*, are old ideas dressed up in new words.
Since we humans need a way to create
understanding in our minds, we often re-create
old, familiar systems under new labels. It gives

us comfort to feel we know what is right, what is wrong, and that what we believe or follow makes sense. It is natural for humans to want to belong, so it is no surprise that those who leave religion behind find themselves falling into the same patterns of thinking—no longer "religious" but "spiritual." Being able to recognize these patterns and how they inform your attitudes and behavior can help reveal what areas of your life need healing. Continually noticing how the ego is leading you instead of the spirit enables you to find these places in your life. Even though the ego may have a bad rap, it plays a very important role—in many ways, guiding us towards safety.

The labels we place on theories or beliefs are not bad. It is the programming that comes through them we must be careful to examine. The teachings are not meant as programs, which is why we must test them and try them through our spirit self to help us understand the energy

behind them, and *how* they are meant to be applied to our lives, if at all.

The ego is the human part of us that protects us. Without it, we are left without an outer shell that forms barriers for survival. It protects us from harm, it warns us, and I believe is the keeper of the spirit. The ego does its job well and our time should not be spent trying to completely rid ourselves of it, but rather train it. Just like any other animal, it is natural for us to react and protect ourselves when we go through something that causes us great distress or harm. In the mental health community or in teachings about trauma responses, this idea is often explained by referring to when humans would need to run away or protect themselves from saber-tooth tigers. This instinct is natural and necessary—we would not survive without it.

I've always found this a funny example as it reminds me of what we do with religious teachings as well—we take something that was a part of the human experience hundreds or thousands of years ago and assume it applies in the same way now. While protection from the tiger is a good example in many ways for describing the purpose of the ego, I think there may be examples we can use that are more culturally relevant for us today.

Composting is one such example or metaphor I will be using in this book. Composting is used by humans to grow a garden or plants, using decayed materials as nourishment for new life, and of course you can find the natural cycle of composting everywhere in nature. Nature is continually using itself to re-create itself, such as a tree composting its own leaves from the previous season. Learning to compost the ego means accepting all aspects of it, allowing those parts no longer needed to fall away and release energy and nourishment which allows the spirit to grow and bear fruit.

This involves training the ego to release the need to be in the lead or in control. It requires a continual regeneration of the primacy of spirit while pruning and releasing unnecessary patterns, then nurturing, caring for, and eventually manifesting new ones that support how the spirit wants to unfold. The nature of spirit is to learn, to become more aware of itself, and to develop a deeper understanding of the energy it comes from. The spirit self is complete and whole in the spirit world, so there is nothing to cause friction for it, to cause it to grow. Coming into the human body and experiencing the obstacles of ego centered life allows spirit to expand and come to know itself as we develop a deeper understanding of who we are and what we are made of.

Those who have spent time in religious settings know the term, "fruits of the spirit." According to the Christian Bible, the fruits of the spirit consist of love, joy, peace, forbearance, kindness, goodness, faithfulness, gentleness, and self-control. The Bible also mentions we must make our bodies our slaves, or circumcise the body, cutting off parts of ourselves that bear bad fruit. In other words, cutting off parts of the ego that cause decay, or stagnate growth; surrendering the parts that do not allow us to come into the knowledge of the true embodied spirit we are; relinquishing the beliefs and thinking that cause us to become stuck in old patterns that need to be transcended. These old energies keep us repeating the same behaviors over and over, hoping to get different results. The ego is convinced that since the behavior worked before, eventually it will meet our current need as well. As long as the ego is in charge, this is how it operates.

But the ego's attempts to protect and problem solve only cut off the flow of spirit, leaving a void beneath. We may even begin to mimic others around us or seek approval and acceptance to fill that void. By becoming aware of these patterns and programmed thoughts, we can discern what needs to be cut away in order to grow. Much like removing a piece of fruit that has become rotten before it causes other fruit to become rotten as well. This is the same process for composting the ego, and what is required in developing the fruits of the spirit.

Because of my religious background and knowledge of the Bible, I have often quoted to myself passages that I hoped would inspire me in my process of spiritual growth, such as this one from *Galatians 5:16. But I say, walk by the Spirit, and you won't fulfill the lust of the flesh.*

Unfortunately, in my programmed mindset I would often use this verse to beat myself up, pushing myself towards an unattainable perfection or trying to keep myself on track from doing something wrong. I would quote the verse to remind myself that I must walk "by the spirit" in order to stay pure and avoid sin and temptations. I had the deep belief I was bad, that I needed to be saved. I was constantly striving to be better. It is not bad to want to be better, but when working out of a perfectionism, fear, or even comparison mindset, it can cause great damage to one's self worth and beliefs about the world. It is my view this kind of striving actually causes the ego to rule with even more rigidity. Perfectionism and fear often lead to feelings of shame. Living a life in shame does not lead to freedom.

Shameful thoughts of being a sinner amplify thoughts that are developed through coping with trauma. As I became more aware of how the spirit works, I began to understand some of these original teachings in a much different way. One of the realizations I came to was that by striving to be rid of the ego's control, or become "sinless," I was causing more resistance to the spirit self by the negative self-thoughts, and beliefs that caused me to want to strive to get rid of certain parts of myself. The more I tried to change myself, the more negative my thoughts became, and the more I was allowing the ego to increase, many times amplifying the exact things I was hoping to rid myself of.

The striving to be "good enough" creates an imbalance between the spirit and ego, which in turn can amplify the ego's need to protect itself and bolster its defenses. To decrease the ego, you must release the resistance to its existence in the first place. This understanding goes against everything we are taught about growth and healing. We are taught by society it is only by hard work that we become better, not by trusting, accepting, and simply reprogramming the mind.

After my dad died, he came to visit me in several visions.[1] This often happened in the mornings, which is a common time for spirits to communicate since the mind is yet to be ruled

---

[1] I recommend going back and reading my first book, *Leaf Lessons*, to understand more about the visions I had and how they played a part in my awakening.

by the ego's processing of the day ahead. One morning my dad came and spoke of what it is like on the other side. He said, "Ang, there is nothing, no one, or anything on this earth that you should be that upset or worried about. Because when you get to this side, the only thing that truly matters is love." Prior to this moment, the only ideas I had about the place we call heaven were those that had been planted in me by the church. Those involved a God in heaven ready to judge us for all the wrongs we commit in our lifetime, and how no one would make it there without accepting Jesus as their savior and living a sinless, pure life. But after this vision and many others, I slowly began to break away from this thinking. I stopped caring so much about all the small things in my life that I held onto so tightly—the inconveniences, the dramas, what other people thought or said, and the need to show up in the way others desired me to (especially the supposed need to be "sinless"). Suddenly everything I had been striving for became less important. Knowing that love was all that mattered helped me see that constantly putting pressure on myself to be perfect was only amplifying negative beliefs about myself and the world around me; it allowed me to see what areas of my life needed to be released and pruned. From this place of love as the priority, I was also able to begin the journey of healing from the traumas I held deep within me, the scars that kept me in cycles of self-defeat and broken relationships.

As I continued to expand in my understanding of love, I began to develop deeper insights into the energy we hold in our bodies, how that energy manifests in our beliefs, which then turn into behaviors, including how we treat ourselves and others. I developed a new understanding of the teachings in the Bible. I realized that when Jesus spoke about the Kingdom of Heaven being within, he was really teaching us about this process of connecting with our own spirit, which emerges directly from the source, which in human understanding is God, the "I Am." We are not separate from the "I Am." And we are also "I Am."

When Jesus was asked if he was "The Son of God," his answer was simply, "I Am." He did not expand on this, did not explain it, didn't create a dogmatic religious idea around the words. He just said it, very simply. The religious leaders were horrified, lashing out in anger, calling it "Blasphemy!" They did not understand the truth behind what Jesus was teaching and why. They didn't know they also were the sons of God.

Buddha taught similarly about the connection within. By extensive trial and error he came to the conclusion that ascetic striving and self-abusive methods to achieve enlightenment were not aligned with truth. When asked about his newfound understanding of the world around him and the spirit within, he simply said, "I am awake." Both Jesus and Buddha reached the point where they were able to use the teachings they had received from the world around them and the experiences they had gone through to compost the old parts of the ego and begin to understand themselves in an enlightened way. Being awakened and connected with the source that created them, both came to realize their true identity as "I am." This is what we are seeking to do as well. It is achievable if we release the hold our egos have on us.

Each person is fully capable of finding their way back to their true source within themselves, of awakening the knowledge that each human is a spirit, made of the same energy from which they are created. The process of decomposing old beliefs involves letting go of the need to be "good," or to be sinless, or pure. As you release these old thoughts and behaviors you begin to understand that striving itself is what keeps us in performance-based behaviors, stress, anxiety, and even hate in our hearts towards other humans. Through the practice of connecting with the spirit over and over, the ego's hold becomes weaker, and the energy of love becomes stronger, which in turn raises the frequency of the person practicing.

I love the moon. Since as far back as I can remember, I always felt connected to it. I wish I could see it more clearly, touch it, understand its energy, and spend my nights watching it as it moves through the night sky. One night during a full moon, I remember walking outside in my backyard to look for it as I normally do when it's full. That night it was hidden behind some trees, not yet fully risen. I looked up and I noticed how clear the whole sky appeared. Normally, being around city lights, I was unable to see the night sky so clearly, the stars and planets and radiance of the moon's light. But in that moment, from where I was standing, I saw it all, and my mind filled with gratitude and wonder.

An overwhelming feeling and awareness came over me that I was not just looking out at this space, but it was also a part of me. I was *this*! All of the beauty, the moon's light, the energies, the brilliance of the universe—WE are IT! Because of my very limited perspective at that moment I could only understand what I was thinking and seeing through my very small lens. In order to expand my understanding, I would need to take the time to move from the position I was in so I could see it from a different perspective.

Many of us become so stuck on the perspective we have that we are not even aware of the possibility to look at things from a different viewpoint. The ego keeps us stuck in the program we developed to survive, continually cycling those same beliefs and assumptions over and over, instead of stepping out in curiosity, exploring new ideas. That night, however, I found myself in complete awe and wonder at how my spirit was connected with everything and everyone around me—a perspective I would not have been open to prior to composting my ego's assumptions about God being something separate from myself. As everyone else was in their homes, or moving about their own lives, I stood there watching the stars, planets, and the moon in orbit; all moving perfectly together, each having its place, and rotating as it was created to do. I saw each part of the night sky providing energy to the earth and the earth back to it—working together, as one. In this energy exchange life is created, humanity, spirit, earth, and all the energies seen and unseen. At that moment, for the first time, I understood what Jesus was trying to teach us about being the "I Am."

The teachings handed down to us as guidance by Jesus communicated these truths. He taught how to walk in our spirit, connect with our consciousness, and understand that we are also the "I Am," that our humanity, even the ego self in its entirety, is connected and one with the great source of energy we call God. Our energy connects with the earth's surface just as the earth's surface connects to ours, and all of it is connected together with the entire universe.

Unfortunately, somewhere along the progression of human thoughts and the development of hierarchical systems, these teachings were hijacked and twisted to become toxic, ruled by the ego, disregarding the truth of enlightenment. Because the thoughts and words we speak manifest our conscious reality, we humans ourselves created the barriers between the ego and spirit and created areas of darkness that disconnected us from our spirit self. This darkness is what impacts our perceived outlook on ourselves and the world around us, and creates the thoughts that manifest the behaviors that influence our lives and the environment we live in. It is here we find the need to compost the programming of the ego, and the cycle of toxic energies, into new understanding which will allow the manifestation of love, and the reconnection with spirit. This is the beginning of learning to walk in the spirit, diminishing the ego's power to rule our lives and manifest our reality. The more we release our current perception and bias, the more able we are to grow in our ability to connect with the "I am" within ourselves.

Chapter 2

Cycle of Life

Nature is constantly composting itself. This is the cycle of life. Trees and other plants are donors helping create other plants, spreading seeds and birthing new things on the earth. There is so much science behind the continued cycle of life on the earth and how plants grow that it would take an entire book to really dig in and explain it. But this is not a book about the scientific cycle of life in nature—I am not an expert in this area and will not pretend to be. However, I intuitively understand how this cycle relates to the human experience. Plants need sun, water, and soil to grow. It is amazing that something we consider so beautiful must grow planted in something we consider "gross." Dirt! I am often struck by this as I watch my own plants grow, tending to them, watering them, placing them in areas with just enough sunlight or shade.

If you travel much, you may have noticed how not all dirt looks the same. If you drive from the state of Kansas down to Oklahoma, you'll see that the dirt changes from a dark, almost black color, to brown, and then a reddish color. The soil changes based on the location and environment, and nourishes different plants. You are not likely to see a palm tree in the Midwest states of the US, yet near coastal areas or deserts you can see a multitude of them. The entire earth is covered in dirt, yet what it's made of and what plants it supports changes according to the location, emitting different frequencies accordingly.

This dirt creates not only plants, but all life, including our own human species. Even humans are connected to the environment, which impacts how we grow. Where we are "planted" influences our understanding of the world around us. The culture we live in develops our beliefs and how we treat other humans. All of it formed out of the environment we come from.

When composting our ego, just like plants use dirt, we use the lessons we learn from life to mold our thinking and beliefs. By composting these lessons, we learn the process of how to use the old to manifest the new. Pruning, releasing, growing. In my first book I shared a vision I had of a leaf in a stream, stuck behind a rock, unable to go with the flow—this is a good metaphor for how our environments and beliefs can keep us stuck from moving forward in life. Staying in one place, fighting the same battles, stuck in our own limited beliefs, not fully releasing the old and stepping into the new. When we only embrace what we consciously know, and neglect to look both outward and inward, we don't see what needs to be pruned. In this stagnant energy we allow our ego to lead, stunt our growth, and stay stuck in areas of our lives we may not necessarily enjoy.

The image of nature's cycle of life offers us a symbolic way to understand what it means to be born again. Each time there is a release of the old, allowing it to decompose, a new creation can come forth. Just like a plant must release parts of itself to stay healthy and grow, we humans must do so as well. To become "reborn," we must continually be releasing, letting go, growing, and flowing. This cycle repeats over and over. Disconnected from these cycles in nature, we also lose touch with our own needs for growth, healing, and releasing. We spend much of our lives unaware of our own cycles.

Without pruning or releasing, plants become withered, sick, or infested. One bad part can cause the rest to become sick as well, causing the plant to die. Therefore, continual pruning of the old helps produce growth. Like plants, our egos become full of toxic energies and destructive thinking that can cause negative or false beliefs, unwanted behaviors, and thinking that can be destructive. If we do not take the time to inventory and rid ourselves of these old energies, beliefs, and programming, we can begin to create more negative energies, thinking, and behaviors that can be harmful for ourselves and others.

The vision of the leaf I shared in the first book is an example of how this happens. Instead of releasing and flowing with the stream, the leaf became stuck behind rocks, fighting against them until it learned to relax and let go. The lesson of the rock in the stream was to teach the leaf how resting and releasing would allow it to flow towards healing, just as releasing the ego's control would allow the spirit's flow. I have come to understand that part of the lesson of the leaf is learning not only to let go of old things that are keeping us stuck, but also to deconstruct and decompose even things we may see as positive in our own nature that keep us from growing. We cannot fully move forward if we hold onto old parts of ourselves, or the decayed negative parts. The story of the past will always come with us, but by composting it as a lesson, it is transformed from being a part of our current narrative to fuel for our ongoing journey.

Spending time pruning our own egos allows us to release the old narrative we developed and step into the new, creating a new story about our lives. Without the knowledge of what needs to be pruned, we can become stuck in the programs and egoistic thinking we may not even realize we are experiencing. In some cases, our ego can even swell, full of self, becoming selfish, defensive, and judgmental. When this happens, we begin to think with our logical egotistic mind, and our programmed beliefs form barriers to love being expressed within our energy. Instead of evaluating the ego and challenging ourselves to see areas in which we may be wrong, we shut ourselves off from others. In order to work through these moments when our human ego becomes stronger than the spirit self, there must be a deep awareness of what needs pruning and composting and a letting go of the stories that limit us, developing instead a relationship within based on compassion and self-love.

During a meditation I was seeking answers from my guides about what it meant to be a human. What exactly does it mean to live on earth? Why human life? I am sure many of us have had these thoughts. The human experience is so complex and strange, especially from the ego perspective. It appears as if we are only here to live our lives servile to a system—creating cycles in our lives, doing the same things every day, and living in the same mindsets, often forming beliefs around our lack of worth, inadequate abilities, and our struggles, even our life purpose.

I know there was time I had the belief I would never do anything greater than what I was doing at the moment. In many ways I believed I had reached my potential in life and there was nothing more for me. Many people reach these moments and spend the rest of their lives in the same place with no awareness they can change it. Staying in the same job, around the same people, in the same home or town. Doing the same behaviors day after day. Believing they are not worth more, can do nothing else, or fearing failure if they try anything outside of that comfort zone. But exploring outside of our set assumptions is beneficial and needed for growth. Without expanding our awareness outside the walls we build around our lives, we are swallowed up by our own thoughts and habits, creating barriers that keep us stuck. Without a sense of existing as spiritual beings, many people never gain understanding of what life itself is all about. Why *this* human experience?

During this meditation, as I was seeking more awareness about why we spirits come to experience human life, I had an experience very similar to the one I shared in my first book, *Leaf Lessons*. The room became full of light, and I stepped out of my human body into an even brighter light. As I traveled out of my body during this meditation, I saw things from a different perspective, from what I would call a universal view. It was as though I was up in space, looking down at the earth. The earth was beautiful, full of light, and the atmosphere around me was full of stars, planets, and the whole cosmos. I could see and feel all the energy. It was so overwhelmingly beautiful there are no words to describe it. I began to float farther from the earth, turning and looking back at it. As I did, I noticed the earth was surrounded by light, almost rainbow-like. As I looked closer, I saw all the living things on earth surrounded by light as well, all of it connected. Every tree, blade of grass, animal, human, plant, even the dirt, was all one field of light. I was in awe.

Slowly, I came to the realization that we humans are the ones who create the dark energies on the earth, through our egos. Because of our ego's stored negative experiences, we form an understanding of the world based on those lower energies and forget about the energies of the spirit. Thus, we create more darkness and then fixate on it.

As my spirit continued to rise into the upper realms, I moved into another layer of energy that felt much different. It was an overwhelming feeling of love so intense and unconditional that I began to sob. Again, there are no words to describe it; I was absorbed in complete awe of this abundant energy, and the enormous amount of love I felt. I realized this was truly where my spirit came from. As I moved into this next realm, I began to see what appeared to be stars all around me, all connected to each other as light, much like what I saw on the earth. I was filled with a deep understanding that there was energy holding everything together as one.

I focused my eyes to look closer at these tiny stars and realized that they were not stars but spirits! I felt a connection of love with each and every one of them, marvelous and beautiful. The spirits moved all around me, and just above me to the right, I noticed a very bright light, huge, more marvelous than the sun. It was white in color but appeared to have all colors in it like a faint rainbow. I did not see a human form, face, or body, only energy, but as I looked at this energy the only word that came to me was "everything." Everything was this and nothing was without it. Eternal, never ending—all!

I kept my gaze on this large mass of energy, overwhelmed with love, and I began to see what appeared to be tiny little stars shooting out of this energy, as if this energy was releasing tiny parts of itself into the atmosphere. As I watched this happen, I focused deeper, becoming intrigued at what I was seeing and what these small dots of light were. I then noticed that each little shooting star that came from this energy was a spirit. Each created and formed out of this enormous energy, in its exact image. It was then I became overwhelmed with the knowledge that THIS was God, and THIS was what it meant to be created in God's image. Each spirit was a direct emanation of what it was created from— an exact reflection and image! As this realization came over me, I once again began to cry with the overwhelming sensations of this knowledge. There was nothing more beautiful than this energy, and the creation coming from it. Each and every spirit was so complete, divinely made, whole, and a direct reflection of love itself.

As I came to the end of this meditation, I did not want to leave this energy and the love I felt. Much like many of my meditations, it was so beautiful I never wanted to be separated from it again. I felt at home. Connected. One with "everything." As I came back into my body, I suddenly understood that my ego body was not what resembled the likeness of God. It's just a vessel which embodies the spirit made from this energy, a protective shell given to us so as to be able to embody in the lower realms. To get back to this understanding of our true origins, it requires cultivating love within, and decreasing the ego body's barriers keeping us from it. We must take all the lessons learned in the human life experience and compost them, using them to grow into the likeness, love, and knowledge of God. Our humanness, the ego, is not the true self. Yet our ego is just as important on earth as our spirit is. Just as all the tiny spirits were connected in the energies above, we here on earth are all connected by energy, divinely created out of light, energy, and love. Through the ego and body, we each express part of this source energy, allowing it to experience itself through countless individual journeys, coming more and more into the understanding of what love really is.

The energy in the heavens is love. But this love is nothing like what we experience in our human egos. If we were to try to describe it, it would take every single positive exclamation and word we can come up with to do so. Love, joy, peace, kindness, happiness, laughing, crying, sex, everything and every positive experience and emotion happening all at once! Nothing in the human body can provide this feeling outside of connection with the spirit.

We only get small glimpses of this in our humanness—when we have a loving or enjoyable feeling or engage in a behavior or activity that creates pleasure in our body. The reason for human life, why we choose to experience earth through human life, allowing all the dirt we experience to help us grow, is to come back into the knowledge of what we are created from, what we hold within, the abundance of love and bliss. Decomposing the ego, learning from the lessons we have in life, experiencing and opening our hearts to pain, hurt, sorrow, and allowing all of it, helps us expand in our understanding of love, learning God's love over and over again.

We humans have forgotten this, becoming trapped in our egos, which disconnect us from our spirit self. We have allowed the darkness created by the ego to become our main focus, always fighting against the barriers in life and forgetting to embrace the abundance of what we have access to. Coming to the knowledge of the All in All, the everything, we must release the resistance and darkness we create with the ego self. The more we do this, the more awareness we come to and connect with our sub-consciousness, developing a true understanding that we are all one. We are this energy working our way back to our spirit, learning to manage the ego, and releasing into the flow. Releasing and flowing as if a leaf in a stream. Becoming a part of the "I am."

Chapter 3

Energy

Scientists have come to understand that everything we see as a solid is actually made up of tiny particles of energy—even our own bodies. In mathematics there is even a way to calculate the surface energy of a solid item. It is mind-blowing to consider a desk I am using, or a chair I am sitting on as more precisely energy than a solid. If I were to take off the lens of my accepted notions, looking through my spiritual eyes instead, I would be able to see this without the need of a scientific explanation. Spirits are also energetic beings and can manifest themselves as more or less solid in relation to human bodies. Those who saw Jesus after his death, likely saw his spirit and not his human body. The records of this return describe him as able to walk through walls and appear before people without notice, which makes sense from an energetic perspective. Spirits are more fluid than what we consider to be material objects, so they can move through them. No wonder this was such a marvelous sight to those who witnessed it, believing he came back from the dead.

Those who are gifted with the ability to see spirits and communicate with them are attuned to the energy spirits are made of, and able to accept that the laws of physics are unable to contain them. There was a time I was skeptical about so-called "psychic" abilities—until I began to experience it myself. I now believe deep in everyone's subconscious is an ability to connect with such intuitive abilities, loved ones who have died, and/or their spirit guides. Until one has developed the ability to quiet the mind and sink into the subconscious of the brain, it is easy to misunderstand the concept of connecting with the spirit world or communicating with them.

When I first learned about spirit guides, I spent a lot of time wondering how to get in touch with them. I knew that my dad had visited me in spirit many times, but I was not aware that I also had guides I could connect with. The first time I was able to connect with my guides I was sitting in my living room playing meditation music in order to set the tone and quiet my mind. It was morning, and I had a small window of time before I needed to be at work. I turned the music on, sat and got quiet, taking a few deep breaths, and grounding myself. I then called out loud for my guides to come and meet with me.

Immediately, I felt the energy of the room shift and an aching pressure around my head. For a moment I was afraid, remembering all the religious warnings about demonic possession. But as this fear arose, so did something else, as if pushing the fear aside—a voice that sounded like my own, saying, "Your energy is too low, you must raise your vibration and energy to meet ours, so your body does not react to the frequency change." On hearing this, I became aware of my own energy, and concentrated on raising its vibration to meet that of my guides. As this frequency changed, my head released the pressure and the ache diminished within seconds.

Once I realized I had changed my own frequency I had to resist getting too excited by this newfound ability so I could stay focused on my guides. As I tried to tune in and listen to them, I received another message that said, "You cannot hear us." I thought it strange that I heard the message, but it was saying I could not hear. I questioned the voice and asked why I could not hear. The voice said, "You cannot hear us because your music is too loud."

I remembered I had my phone with the meditation music playing on it sitting right beside me. I reached over, found the volume button, and turned the music down a bit, but still loud enough it would continue to help me feel "spiritual." I returned my attention to my energy and my guides and tuned back in to see if I could get a message. Again, they said, "Your music is to loud." Frustrated, I reached back over and turned the volume down some more, but not all the way down because I assumed the atmosphere of the room needed to have some kind of "spiritual vibe" to meet spirit guides. (That's what we always did in church to make things feel spiritual—have music on). Once again, I returned my focus and tried to hear from my guides. This time I was told, "You cannot hear us. Turn the music off. You don't need music to be spiritual!"

At this, I began to laugh hysterically because I finally realized that the whole time I was trying to hear from my guides, I was being driven by my ego's programmed beliefs that I needed to do something to "be good enough" to be in touch with such highly spiritual beings. As I began to laugh, I sensed that my guides were laughing with me, which made me laugh even harder that I could cause my guides to laugh. I finally turned the music off completely, telling my guides that they would need to remind me of the time so I would not be late for work, as I had set my phone to end the music at the time I needed to leave.

After we had a chuckle about my ego trying to control this moment, I turned my energy back in and asked, "How many of you are there?" I heard a faint voice that sounded much like mine say, "Six." I thought to myself, *Wow! SIX! That is a lot.* A picture formed in my head of six energies standing before me. They did not have human bodies but appeared as energies each outlining a human body. As these energies stood before me, all in a row, I suddenly sensed an excited spirit pop its head up between two of them and say, "SEVEN! SEVEN! I'm a guide too!" I thought, *DAD!?? Is that you?* This new spirit excitedly moved to the end of the line of guides, and I sensed a smile as I heard, "I'm one of your guides too." Then, "Well, I'm just the guy in training, these are your real guides, but I am one too!" Clearly it was my dad's spirit. He had the same personality as he did on earth, silly and goofy, always making me laugh in some way. I was glad to know my dad was playing an active role in helping to guide my life.

As the exchange went on between myself and my guides, we spent much of the time laughing together. Then I suddenly heard, "We're done." And just like that, the energy shifted. I turned to look at my phone's time, only to discover we had ended at the exact minute I had set the music to end. It was an experience I would never forget.

That moment gave me a lot of insights about my energy and the energy of the spirit world. For one thing, my energy was a much lower frequency than that of my guides. The more work I do to decrease my ego's need to rule my mind and body, the more I am able to increase my energy to stay in close relationship with my guides. I also learned that spirits of loved ones who have transitioned embody the same personality and energetic frequency they held as a human, just more enhanced and pure.

As I learned more about this domain, I heard a lot of different descriptions of how guides or spirits looked to others. Most of them appeared in human or even animal form recognizable to the human mind. I wondered for a long time why I did not have the same kind of impressions, only experiencing or seeing their presence as energy, rather than as familiar physical bodies. One day I was given the insight by my guides that spirits do not have a form, and when one does present itself as a human or animal, it is simply a way to help the human mind that is connecting with them to feel comfortable with and make sense of what they are seeing. As we gain experience connecting with and aligning more with our own spirit, we become more familiar with the spirits we communicate with and how fluid they are in form. This in turn helps us understand the nature of our own spirit. Ordinarily, seeing only the outside of things through our surface mind, we are not aware that deep within us is our true source of energy. The more we become aware of energy as the real substance of things, the more we come into alignment with our subconscious.

If we could truly see things as they were, we would see marvelous energy all around us. Instead, with our human mind we create illusions and interpretations based on wrong views, convincing ourselves that what we physically see is all that is real. Some call this illusion the "matrix." Deep down inside of us, we know that what we can see with our human eyes is not the whole truth, that the very thing in front of us is only a mirage caused by the programmed ego mind, but even so we believe it without question. Through our ego conditioning we develop assumptions about how the world operates, limiting ourselves to what we physically see. Religious teachings create even more confusion, dismissing scientific discoveries about energy and the mysterious properties of our physical world as something to be avoided all together. As a Christian I was taught that science disconnects us from God and leads us to worship material things around us instead of the 'real' God, who is assumed to be separate from us. In this type of thinking we forget that we ourselves are part of the vast field of energy that includes galaxies, stars, planets, and things yet to be discovered by the human eye. To dismiss the discoveries that come from science about this energy only further disconnects us from our own selves.

During one meditation I experienced a small glimpse of this immense field of energy. I began to have a vision of the earth throughout its billions of years in existence, and how it compares to the evolution and progress of humans. I saw the earth as a living organism, continually changing and raising the quality of its frequency. Just within my lifetime I have seen amazing creations and developments that use energy in ways I myself will never be able to understand—the fact that I can carry a device that connects me with other humans at any moment, anywhere I desire, is something those who lived thousands of years ago could not have imagined. Because the human mind has come to understand how to manipulate and use energy, we have been able to harness it for our own benefit in many ways. If this energy is so powerful that we can use it to connect with one another on a small device, imagine how influential and abundant the energies in and around us truly are. The human mind cannot comprehend it, but spirit can. Jesus understood this when he answered a questioner about whether he was God in the flesh, saying simply, "I am."

Through spiritual awakening you develop the understanding that there is a clear difference between your spirit and ego. Our spirit is love, connected to all the energies around us, fully at peace. The ego is also energy connected to all things; however, it is ruled by the mind's programming. The goal of human life is to decrease the ego's hold on us and increase our connection with the spirit—as if we are working to merge the two into one, the yin and yang, both having a purpose and function, separate, yet one. I believe this is the reason each of us decided to come into this human experience: to merge the spirit and ego by building a connection between them, then working to allow the spirit to lead. Without the ego becoming exposed to the spirit over and over, through practices such as meditation, the ego continues to rule, holding onto toxic energies and reflecting only itself.

The ego has a legitimate job, which is to protect the individual human life. Many don't understand that the ego is not an enemy to defeat, but a part of the same energy as the spirit. However, the ego, being developed through lower vibrations of energy (as my guides explained to me), is in need of training. Our experiences in life, including traumas, all get energetically stored in the body. These stored energies can influence the body and mind, developing negative behavior patterns, a scarcity mindset, barriers to maturity, mental illness, or physical sickness. They also decrease the ability to connect with our sub-consciousness and intuition. Being able to clear these energetic patterns allows the spirit to take the lead and decrease the ego's defensive responses to triggers, which allows us to become more authentically connected with our true self.

The mind is connected to the body and the body is connected to the mind, and all of this is connected to the spirit. Without clearing out the toxic energies we hold in our bodies, the energy of trauma continues to cycle through the mind, maintaining the thinking and behaviors which keep us stuck. This explains why some people may struggle with things such as anger outbursts, pain in the body, addictions, lack of self-awareness, and even narcissistic tendencies.

The body has many parts, but functions as a whole. The heart and brain keep the body alive. If either one stops working, life does not continue in the body. However, without the spirit, the body ceases to remain alive as well. It all works together. The spirit keeps the body alive, the brain keeps the heart pumping, the heart circulates the blood, and it all repeats and recycles. The cycle of life. All of it working as one. This body creates an energetic barrier between the lower frequencies of earth and the higher frequencies of our spirit. When we hold toxic energies in the body, or if the energy is stagnant and unclear, this will manifest as sickness in the body or mind, or it will create other blocks keeping us from connecting with our higher self and manifesting something new. To manifest something new, old energy needs to be cleared first, and this requires we become aware of the energy we currently hold within.

Deep inside, all of us desire to love and be loved. Love is our true nature because love is the nature of our spirit. That is why when we get in touch with our spirit, we are getting in touch with love. This is also why one of the first things you must learn in order to clear your energy is to love yourself. Our ego's beliefs about the self are based on past experiences and programming we received from others around us in childhood, which in turn is a direct reflection of the way they perceived themselves, and so on. Each of us projects onto others what we hold for ourselves, and in this way, we pass along negative ideas or misperceptions across generations.

To release the stuck energies that no longer serve us, it is beneficial to begin to pay attention to our thoughts, and to see them as forms of energy. Many of these thoughts are beliefs from past experiences and possible traumas we experienced, and are no longer relevant now. Seeing them for what they are begins the process of breaking them down. Just as most living things on the earth compost and repurpose old or dead parts, we can use the lessons we learn through our egos as compost to fuel growth as well. This process increases our understanding of love and the ability to manifest it in our lives. Even through hard or negative life experiences we develop the ability to love more and become more empathic towards others. Many of the experiences we face in life can be used to connect our ego with the spirit, by increasing our understanding of love.

Pain is often a signal, reminding us of our purpose and revealing the things we need to compost or prune from our lives. Through both dark and joyous moments, we learn more about love. Think of the experience a mother has when birthing a child and how they experience both pain and joy in the process. Though the birth is painful for the mother, once it is complete, the experience usually ends with blissful joy. This can create in the mother a deeper understanding of love for another human. This is a perfect example of how hard moments have the potential to manifest the greatest gifts of our lives, outweighing the pain of events or experiences we had, exposing the beauty in them.

However, without knowledge of how to clear or manage energy, the person going through such a difficult event risks becoming stuck with the energy, whether positive or negative, creating circular thinking, ruminating over the event, or continually manifesting the same behavior over and over in their daily lives, unable to move on. An extreme form of this is PTSD from a negative event or series of events, such as a veteran returning from war, who lives with recurring nightmares, reliving the energies created on the battlefield, triggered by otherwise insignificant stimuli into outbursts of rage, or crippled by anxiety.

On the other hand, an example of a more "positive" form of this would be a parent so consumed by the ecstatic feelings of love they have for their child, and how the child's innocence makes them feel, that they form an inappropriate attachment to the child, using it to fill their own void, to alleviate their own pain or need for self-love. This puts an unhealthy burden on the child to show up for the parent instead of the other way around, and the child may even feel responsible for their parent's feelings of disappointment or lack of self-esteem. They don't have any way of understanding that it is the parent's responsibility to develop the love they seek within themselves.

The ironic result of the parent not loving themselves is that the child learns the same thing. The parent's unmet needs prevent them from expressing love for their child in a healthy way. If this is not addressed, such a child, once grown, can spend their lives seeking unsuccessfully to feel loved by others, or behaving in ways that are not authentic in order to "earn" the love they feel they are missing. Some even find themselves in unhealthy relationships and yet stay in them because it is familiar, the energy they hold within resonates with someone else that is also disconnected from themselves.

This cycle is endless: not loving oneself, seeking to feel loved by others, altering one's persona or behavior to try to get love, trying to fill the void unsuccessfully in these ways, then believing one is not worthy of love, and so on. This is how the energy of codependency is created. Giving another the responsibility to make us feel loved breaks down healthy energetic boundaries and causes loss of self-respect and dignity.

Codependency leaves one persons' sense of self-worth entirely dependent on another. Typically, this involves putting your own needs on the back burner to prioritize somebody else's. Many who have been through childhood trauma struggle with this in some form. It takes self-awareness, growth, and even more understanding of the need for self-love to begin to break away from this type of energy. Part of composting the ego is letting go of the behaviors that keep us stuck in these cycles and learning how to set healthy boundaries.

Many adults struggle with boundaries as they were never taught to be separate beings from their parents in a healthy way, especially if their parents also experienced significant trauma themselves. Because the energy of codependency can create a toxic cycle, it creates barriers in the energetic field that keep us from moving freely into our sub-conscious spirit and connecting with our intuition. We may even explain away red flags or warning signs of toxic energies in us or in others. We can convince ourselves that we are responsible for the love another feels for themselves, or we can create stories around events as if they describe who we are as a person, holding onto the same narrative throughout our lives, repeating self-limiting stories or staying in abusive cycles. Cycles of abuse can remain in families for generations before someone becomes aware of it and breaks out of it.

Looking outside ourselves for love can even be seen in religious communities that emphasize a reliance on a God instead of ourselves or focus on how we are seen by others through the outward appearance of faithful acts. Religion can also cause us to be overly concerned about the process of making it to heaven, forming a codependency with Jesus (or another savior figure) as we assume that our actions impact whether he loves or accepts us. This is how we disconnect our ego from our spirit, by focusing outwardly on gaining the approval of someone, even a man who lived thousands of years ago.

Seeking love outside of ourselves, we are less likely to go inward to seek the guidance of our spirit, connect to our intuition, or build self-love. Seeking love outside ourselves disconnects us from our truth and creates dependency, as we forget the source of love is the spirit within.

If we allow our experiences in life to help us build a deeper connection and relationship with our own selves, we have the increased ability to connect with the spirit within us and in this place, we find deep healing for our ego. Healing can happen in many forms, but it is through developing a deep connection with self that we truly are able to heal. The traumas, experiences, and cycles we hold in our energy and body are what keep us disconnected from self, and we continue to seek things outside of ourselves such as food, addictions, or the approval of other humans to fill the void. When we form relationships that are not based on self-love, these attachments can actually create barriers for us to receiving love as well as to loving them fully. Just as Jesus taught us, love your neighbor as you love yourself. The first lesson of the ego is to learn self-love, the second, how to radiate that love outwards into the world around us, towards others. This is what true connection with self and others really is.

Chapter 4

Reflections

Most of us go through life without really looking in the mirror and seeing our own reflection clearly. Many of us avoid the mirror altogether, quickly looking away before we can see ourselves. Filled with shame and self-hatred we would rather not see who we think is there. If we do look at all, it is usually to correct something, judge ourselves, or modify our image and cover our flaws to present something we think will be acceptable to the world. There is a verse in the Bible that talks about looking in the mirror. I have come to see it in a different light since I have become more awakened to my spirit self.

But be doers of the word, and no only hearers, deluding your own selves. For if anyone is a hearer of the word and not a doer, he is like a man looking at his natural face in the mirror; for he sees himself, and goes away, and immediately forgets what kind of man he was.
The World English Bible; James 1:22-24-27

I believe the message is referring to not seeing our spirit self. We have forgotten who we are, developing instead an outer facade based on our ego's conditioning. We walk away from our inner spirit's consciousness and think and act with our outward identity, believing the toxic thoughts and beliefs we have about ourselves and the world around us. We avoid the things we do not like about ourselves, and the hard emotions we have stored in our bodies, which causes us to continue to avoid our own reflection, to avoid seeing or feeling our inner spirit or hearing its voice. In this way, we remain stuck in the ego's limited perspective, disconnected from our spirit.

Taking the time to look deep into yourself through meditation allows you to connect with your inner state and truth, which then releases the toxic thoughts and energies from the body that keep us stuck in a negative mindset. But many of us do not take the time to reflect within, which is the only true way to align with what is true about ourselves.

The lesson of looking in the mirror has nothing to do with our physical appearance, and everything to do with what our spirit is here to learn. It refers to looking past our surface selves to see the truth of who we are deep under all the skin, flesh, bones, and all we associate with our limited notion of ourselves. The human body is a beautiful creation made to work together with the spirit to keep it anchored in this lower frequency of energy on the earth. But the body is not to be our main focus in this life.

Spirits are directly connected with their source and exist at a much higher frequency than the material earth's energy, which includes our bodies. Our spirits need the body as a shell to create a barrier and connect them to the material realm. Incarnating as human allows the spirit to experience itself through material form. Our bodies aren't necessarily created in the image of God, it is our spirit that is. Our bodies are created from the earth, as the teaching explains, "From dust we came, to dust we return." Which brings us back to the sacredness of dirt. Maybe we shouldn't work so hard to avoid or look away from the dirt in our own lives. Maybe from all this dirt we get the experience and growth we are seeking.

I have developed a love of crystals over the years, intrigued by how they grow in the ground. I used to be afraid of them, taught by religion that ritual use of anything connected to the earth was tantamount to pagan worship of false gods—giving glory to the created instead of the creator. As I opened my spirit to seeing all things as connected to the same source, I began to see the beauty of the earth in ways I had not before, and understood that it played a significant role in the human experience. Experiencing the energy of crystals has allowed the earth to come into my awareness more, and I believe the energy in them comes from the same source that all things do. I began to use them for connecting with my spirit or helping to heal my body.

Throughout human history, crystals and minerals and other substances (such as Frankincense and Myrrh) were recognized as tools for healing or connecting with the spirit. Even in the Bible many gemstones are mentioned, in particular, the book of Revelations describes the foundation wall of Jerusalem as being decorated with twelve precious stones.

The foundations of the city's wall were adorned with all kinds of precious stones. The first foundation was jasper, the second sapphire; the third chalcedony, the fourth emerald, the fifth sardonyx, the sixth sardius, the seventh chrysolite, the eighth beryl, the ninth topaz, the tenth chrysoprase, the eleventh jacinth, and the

twelfth amethyst. The twelve gates were twelve pearls. Each one of the gates was made of one pearl. The street of the city was pure gold, like transparent glass.
World English Bible; Book of Revelation 21:19-20

During one mediation I had an insight about how each crystal is formed from specific vibrations and energies within the earth. The thought came to me that crystals are formed from the same energy of love that we are when we emerge from the one vast field of light. When our spirits depart our bodies, and the bodies are placed back into the earth to decompose, the spirits leave behind the frequency of their energy which influences the formation of crystals. As this strange thought came over me, I began to imagine that the crystals we dig out of the earth represent the energies of our ancestors that lived long ago. This insight combined with my previous vision of the earth being covered in beautiful light: I was filled with wonder that the soil we stand on is also divine, created for growth and healing, and constantly evolving. These crystals are just a glimpse of the abundant energy of the earth, an expression of the sacred source of its manifestation.

Native Americans have always had a true understanding of how sacred the earth is, giving reverence to the ground and soil that gives them food, the animals as well, and watching the cycles of the sun, moon, and planets and their effects on the earth and its waters, weaving together the energies above and below. They watched these cycles to know when to forage for or grow certain plants, when to use them for medicinal purposes as well as for sacred rituals and for food.

It was from native people's understanding of nature's medicines that modern medications have been derived. But they understood those medicines in a spiritual context. When Europeans colonized the Americas, killing the people and stealing their resources for their own gain and profit, they took the sacred meaning out of them, creating secondary substances with negative frequencies that can cause other sickness. Many ingredients in modern day medications originated from plants originally used by native people, but were copied and synthesized so companies could make more profit from them.

For example, willow bark was widely known by Native Americans to relieve indigestion, act as an anti-inflammatory, and reduce pain. They also used this as a topical for wounds or cuts. European chemists, seeing how effective willow bark was, found that it contains a chemical called salicin, which they believed to be the key ingredient to its effectiveness; they isolated salicin from the willow bark and modified it into a new compound they called salicylic acid, which among other things is the active ingredient in modern-day aspirin tablets. In the same way, a multitude of drugs we now use came from isolating and synthesizing molecules found in effective medicinal plants already in use by people who understood the spiritual and healing powers in the world around them.

When we work to compost the ego, we also find this healing power. In each of us is a healing frequency held deep within our spirit, and in it the ability to heal ourselves, and to help others heal. By doing the work to decrease our ego's control, we come back into the ability to connect with our spirit and this healing energy, allowing our spirit's energy to rise higher. As this process happens, we connect to the same energy sources found in the plants used for healing. This is why it is so important we take time to look in the mirror *past our flaws* to see the abundant energy that is stuck in unhealthy patterns and sickness; by releasing that energy we can connect with the divine beings we are, the spirits in the bodies we currently live in. We truly are magnificent beings, full of healing energy.

As we work to compost our ego and connect with our spirit, doing the work to prune and use the old lessons we go through to help us move forward and learn, we intentionally participate in the cycle of death and rebirth: dying to the old and birthing the new. This is the process that has been expressed in traditions and teachings from masters and wisdom holders throughout human history: we must die to be reborn.

When we take the time to look at our reflection, we will understand the frequency of love we truly embody. Then we begin to connect with our healing powers and abilities. As we do this, we learn how to let go of and move stagnant energies that have kept us from growing and healing, increasing the flow of abundant energies. We release the grip of ego that creates anxiety, hurt, and other lower energies and connect once again with our highest self. The energy of light we each radiate, the image we finally see in the mirror, is that same star that once shot out of the magnificent original energy. We are created in the image of God, and when we take the time to look in the mirror and see this, we finally begin to live the truth of who we are

Chapter 5

Manifesting

I had a dream several years ago that I still remember today. In the dream I was in a home that had a snake in it. In fear, I ran down to the basement to grab something to kill it and get it out of the house. When I got to the basement all I found were several toy garden tools: a tiny plastic shovel, rake, bucket, and other toys a child would use to play in a garden. I went to grab the toy shovel and realized that it would be useless on the snake. I was scared and didn't know what to do, so I started running around in circles trying to get away from the snake. As I ran, the snake started to chase me and became more and more frightening. I couldn't get away from it. Instead of running back up the stairs and outside to get away, I just stayed in the basement running in circles, terrified I was going to die, continuing to be chased by the snake. As the dream came to an end, I heard a voice in my spirit say to me, "You need better tools to protect yourself."

I had forgotten about this dream until recently when working with a new client. I was trying to teach them how to use meditation to connect with their spirit and healing abilities. The client kept coming back with the excuse they could not quiet their mind long enough to meditate because there were many outward distractions keeping them from doing so. The distractions would often take precedence over the inner work that needed to be done for their healing and connection with self.

I realized that the message of the snake dream was that the snake was the ego-mind, the repetitive thoughts in the mind that create fear, and running around in circles was like the loops of overthinking, analyzing, judging, comparing, desperately trying to "figure out" how to stop the snake/the ego-mind of fear and negativity. But instead of trying to run away from the snake, and instead of trying to defeat or control the ego-mind, the solution is to stop and face the mind, the thoughts. Sitting still, being with them, accepting them, is what allows them to finally calm so the spirit can take back the reins and take the lead again.

In my own growth and awakening to spirit, I have come to understand how our wild, untamed minds manifest our realities. I had a really hard time for many years controlling my thoughts and what went through my mind. Whatever programmed beliefs came to mind I believed, whether they were the truth or not. Even in my understanding of spiritual things I followed the crowd I was surrounded by. I would question things once in a while but was always afraid to fully trust my own intuition.

As I went through my spiritual awakening process, my biggest questions were about the concept of hell, wondering if it was a real place and if I was risking going there because I had changed my beliefs about the God I was serving. Previously, I had always believed if I ever wandered from the path I was on, I would be damned to eternal torment. I thought this was what love was. I thought God had to send people to hell if they disobeyed him or didn't follow his son because he was so holy and pure there could be no sin in his presence. I believed this was justice, that even the little babies of the world were born sinners and damned to hell if they were not saved by Jesus, a person who lived thousands of years ago.

I was plagued by thoughts of hell, and the idea that people I loved could be there or were going there. I hoped there would be an end to the world one day, that this place called hell would also be destroyed and those souls would just cease to exist and not be tormented for eternity. Then they would also be free. It was a strange feeling to think that because I had accepted Jesus, I didn't have to worry that I would ever go there. But I was saddened for my friends and family that likely would.

It makes no sense to me now that a loving God would create such a place and send people there just because they don't behave a certain way or believe in his son; that more than two-thirds of the world belonging to other religions or faiths would be going to hell because they didn't have the same thoughts and beliefs as I did; that somehow, the Christians had gotten it right and the rest of the world had it wrong. Thinking back to how these beliefs influenced my thinking and behavior, I am saddened by all the time I spent trying to convince people they were wrong and I was right. Looking back at this, I see I spent more time hurting other humans than loving them. All the fear, heartache, and torment of my belief in this eternal punishment caused me to become prideful and demanding of other people's lives, time, and behavior. Without even realizing it, I was causing my own hellish experience on earth—manifesting my fear into reality, causing disorder between myself and others, and holding onto beliefs that I had to be other than I was to be good enough for love, and projecting that same fear onto others.

The torment in my mind continued for many years until I started to put the puzzle pieces together about what love really is. Real love doesn't cause or wish harm on others. Love does not demand or command. Love is gentle and kind. It allows and releases. It expands and opens. Love flows. Like a leaf in a stream, love does not resist. It just is. You cannot contain love, put it in a bottle, or place a barrier around it. It is our human ego that experiences emotions such as anger and with that energy can hurt ourselves and others. It is these moments of absorption in our own ego that cause us to disconnect with our true nature and resist love. But love does not go away. Love always remains.

*Love is patient and is kind. Love doesn't
envy. Love doesn't brag, is not
proud, doesn't behave itself
inappropriately, doesn't seek its own way,
is not provoked, takes no account of
evil; doesn't rejoice in unrighteousness,
but rejoices with the truth; bears all things,
believes all things, hopes all things, and
endures all things.*

The World English Bible; 1 Corinthians 13:4-7

If God is love, then God is all of these. How can
a God that is this type of love create eternal
torment? Why would a God that is this love
create a place of darkness for its own self, its
own creation?

As I worked through releasing old thinking I
would often mull over these old religious
teachings and thoughts I had about God. I was
trying to figure out if I believed in a place called

hell or if all spirits are truly a direct reflection of what we call God. I came to the conclusion that the negative beliefs were real, but only because I believed they were real. We manifest into our reality what we believe based on what we think in our minds. When I still believed in the religious dogma I'd been taught, I struggled to understand my gift of being able to see and speak with spirits. I assumed that my experiences were demonic and believed that darkness was all around me trying to keep me from God. Even as I was awakening, my friends still in the religion would warn me about demons being able to speak to us, convincing us that things are true that maybe aren't. But the more I came to understand the power of my thoughts, the more I realized that these beliefs were not true.

Many of the darker energies we encounter in our lives are not only due to our thinking, but can be negative energies due to trauma. Trauma is formed out of negative energies held in our bodies and projected back into the world around us, creating the appearance of the darkness we hold within. Instead of seeing this as an energy created through the ego self, we blame it on something outside of ourselves and create stories of hell and demonic activity to explain it.

I am not saying that everything is self-imposed—the reality is that hurtful things happen to people in this world. In my first book, I speak about many things that were hurtful and damaging to me in my life, especially as a young, innocent child. But on top of those experiences, and as part of ego formation, I created a story to explain them, to help me make sense of them; beliefs about myself and the world around me, even creating self-imposed negative beliefs. It is those ongoing beliefs and thought patterns that perpetuate the suffering created by the original trauma. It is true that horrific things happen to people, and people sometimes turn the hate held within themselves outward towards others in the world, perpetuating the cycle of harm. It makes complete sense that we would want some kind of justice for the wrongs done to us, and for these people to experience torment for eternity for their actions.

We often want others to suffer the way they have caused us to suffer. The hardest part of composting the ego is realizing that even those people who hurt us are a reflection of the energy of God we also came from. In our egotistic mind it is easy to believe that there is a need for a place called hell to punish such people. But as much as it feels justified that people would be tortured for their behaviors, we cannot deny they are made of the same energy that we are. It is only that their energy is full of toxic vibrations and evil expressions because of the egotistic thinking that afflicts us all, the darkness created by the human mind. As much as it would give us ease to believe evil people go to hell, I have concluded that there is no such place.

Based on what and how we think, we manifest into our reality what we *believe* to be true. People who have had near death experiences, and describe a hellish experience after leaving the earth, often already believe there is hell. There are plenty of others who have had near death experiences that never described it as hellish at all. Some who experienced the after-life as hellish reflect that they may have created the experience based on their previous beliefs. These individuals also mention they knew how to get out of the hellish experience just by thinking of a different place.

Because the spirit is our true self and is eternal, the shift between the material human experience back into the spirit can be somewhat confusing for our spirits. For example, I recently received a message from one of my spirit guides about how brief our human life really is. There is no time in the spirit world, so our human interpretation of it is based on our ego's limited experience. From the perspective of the spirit, the time spent as a human is relatively insignificant—the equivalent of just seconds.

When we transition into our human experience, we have guides that stay with us for the duration of our life on earth. When we are ready to transition back into the spirit, these guides, often including loved ones who left before us, are waiting to help bring us back into the higher frequencies of the spirit realm. Human life, full of so many different emotions and experiences, clings to the spirit, which can be disorienting as we move back into the higher realms. When we transition, according to many near-death-experiencers, there is a moment of confusion outside of the body, looking back at the body and the scene taking place around it. The idea of being dead doesn't make sense. After this first shock, the spirit begins its transition into the higher dimensions, usually beginning with appearing in a completely dark place. The energy of this place is sometimes described as cocoon-like, feeling safe and held. Sometimes it is described like a waiting room. The spirit remains there until a guide or angel appears, helping them understand that they have left human life and are ready to transition back into spirit. This being then guides us to an even higher realm where we continue to review our life and experience the bliss of true love and joy.

One of my guides explained to me that the transition after death can feel like whiplash because the experience is so different in the spirit than it was in the human body. The spirit needs time to adjust, reflecting on its experiences in human form. Human life is the only place we actually experience any lower energies that can be interpreted as evil or dark. Even in the higher realms we call heaven, the darkness is based on love and support for the spirit, guiding it as it moves between the lower and higher realms.

This got me thinking about the possibility of spirits becoming stuck in between—not fully transitioning back into the higher realms, staying in the holding place and continuing to have interactions with the spirits still having a human experience. I think of when my dad's spirit came to me after he died to talk to me about forgiveness and asking me for forgiveness. According to what my guides explained to me, there is a continued pruning that takes place as a spirit moves higher and higher in frequency. This might include a reckoning with themselves and the impact they had on others during their life. They may desire to make amends with those they harmed, to release them to find their own truth and heal. As spirit, they may recognize the nature of the ego mind, and how the material body stores traumatic energies, and wish to convey this insight to those who are still alive in human form. This can cause some spirits to become stuck in this in-between place. When a spirit presents itself to a living human, they may unfortunately be mistaken for a dark or evil entity.

What we think and believe directly influences
what manifests as our reality. All thoughts
develop, manifest, and are perpetuated in the
ego mind. Because we do not know how to use
the entirety of our brain consciously and
intentionally, the brain often wanders around on
its own in whatever way it has been
programmed, cycling the same thoughts over
and over, recycling the same emotions and
feelings over and over without any awareness. It
is truly amazing how many thoughts we can
have in a day without being aware of any one of
them. We may not even realize we have the
ability to pay attention to our thoughts. Without
question, we believe everything that comes into
our minds. Because we believe what our ego
mind creates, we seek out evidence to prove our
experiences and beliefs (sometimes referred to
as confirmation-bias). The stories we repeat to
ourselves become more and more real to us,

manifesting as more thoughts, beliefs, and behaviors, as well as informing how we interpret others and what goes on around us. We seem to be manifesting the very things we already believe; without realizing it, we are creating the reality we live in. People who continue to have the same struggles no matter what they do, or who experience the same kinds of situations over and over, have no idea how much their own mind is keeping them stuck in those patterns. The exact behaviors we may want to eliminate become our identity. We are quick to want to prove, even defend our limitations or diseases.

The human ego has developed the belief that these negative experiences are the devil's doing—putting blame on something outside ourselves, relinquishing our own responsibility, power, and agency. Instead of taking a look at ourselves and what is programmed in our ego, or how life experiences and the thoughts we have manifest our reality, we make excuses for the behaviors or struggles we have, thereby perpetuating them. Until we become aware of this, we will likely repeat the same feelings, emotions, and behaviors over and over.

In a society that continues to reprogram our minds over and over, creating more fear, more judgment, more racism and belittlement, it is no wonder that the idea of hell and dark spirits is so prevalent in human minds. Our ego knows nothing else. Greed, struggle for success and attention, and the need to be loved by someone outside of ourselves, are all attempts to fill the void in our heart that can only be filled by connecting with our own spirit. It is interesting that the very people striving to prove and defeat darkness are the same ones creating the darkness in their lives themselves. If someone does not agree with their belief about the darkness, they can become defensive and angry, creating even more dark experiences around themselves.

It was not very long ago that I heard in my spirit a message that I hope I never forget. I believe my guides shared something so profound with me that if we truly were able to grasp the magnificence and beauty of it, we would be very protective of our voices and what we speak out into the world. The message I heard was that we have no idea how powerful our voice, words and even vocal tone is. Our voice, just like our fingerprints, eyes, and hair follicles are so very unique that no other person out of the billions on the planet have the exact same tone of voice or sound frequency. If you really take a moment to think about this, you realize the amount of energy we use to speak each day impacts not just yourself, but the lives of others around you. Our voice is so powerful it can manifest and create each day, and we are either using it for good, or to form more darkness on the earth. When we belittle one another, or say hateful words towards others, those sounds create a vibration that moves into the atmosphere and impacts not just ourselves but those around us. Even plants are impacted by the negative words we speak.

Our voices are astonishingly powerful. No other voice is your voice, no other human can speak with your unique vocal tone—how much more power and insight does this give to the idea of our spirit being made in the image of God? God spoke the universe into existence; we also have the ability to manifest through our voice. But absorbed in the low vibrations of earth, we forget this unique power and the responsibility that goes with it, using it unconsciously to create darkness which, in turn, develops a barrier that makes it harder and harder to connect with our truth, and spirit.

Have you ever sat and watched the world population clock? If not, I encourage you to look it up and spend a moment watching it. It is amazing how the numbers so quickly change. There is a daily birth count, a death count, and an overall number of people. While watching this, I've had some startling realizations. One, how many people are truly in the world, and how I am just one person in that vast population. Two, how quickly the population count changes, both up and down. The reason it goes up and down is because there are births and deaths happening at the same time every second. What is even more crazy to think about is, of all the billions of people recorded and living on this earth, not a single one of them makes it out alive. Each one will face goodbye as the people they know leave the earth, and each person will also face their last day as a human on this earth. Following this insight even further, not a single one of those bodies will be lived in again. Another body may have similar features and structure, but it will never be the exact same body.

If our voices, bodies, human design, create such a diverse population on the earth, then no wonder we have so many different beliefs, thoughts, and understandings of the world. All different thinking, all different beliefs, and all formed as a direct reflection of the culture and society we are born in. We truly are beautifully and wonderfully made. With this understanding of the human experience, it makes sense that we ourselves, in our own human ego, create both light and darkness on the earth. If humans represent anything of our creator, there really is nothing to fear and no separation from God, even in the darkness we have created around us.

The spirit that creates our personality, abilities, gifts, desires, and all the positive aspects about us, is the same energy it came from, which we call God. If we took the time to develop a connection in our spirit to this, we would truly understand that nothing can separate us from God's love. If the passage is interpreted correctly, then it can help us begin to break out of the toxic energetic beliefs creating darkness in the world around us. Instead of creating barriers to the abundant love and expansion of our highest self, we would spend time taming our minds, connecting with our spirit, and composting the ego's limiting beliefs into the wisdom that is our true nature.

This is what the dream of being chased by the snake was trying to covey. The snake represented the ego creating fear and darkness through habitual, repetitive thoughts—over analyzing situations, trying to control them, judgement towards others, and the never-ending looping thoughts of our minds keeping us in anxiety and fear. Through mindfulness and meditation we learn to turn and face our ego-mind, the snake, instead of running away from it. When we can face the ego, it loses its power over us, becomes tame; then we can reconnect with love, with our true selves, and live life aligned with our spirit.

Chapter 6

Darkness

I am going to introduce a radical insight about darkness that may be hard to understand for those still working to connect with the subconscious. We humans are the ones who create the darkness on the earth. Everything created within the human experience is a direct reflection of our thoughts manifesting into reality. The energy of darkness is included. What is interesting about this process is that even though we have a part in developing the darkness, we also fight against it. We place blame on a source outside of ourselves for creating it, then try to eradicate it "out there," which misses the point. In many ways, the darkness serves a purpose in human life. Some of the darkness comes from generations prior to us, and even from many thousands of years prior to when we walked the earth. But if you have any spiritual understanding of the cycle of life, you will develop some insight into how some of the same energies that created the darkness long ago are also still circulating the earth today.

Darkness is one of those subjects that we either want to avoid altogether, or we want to explore it, perhaps to find out what causes it. It is also possible to find enjoyment from the feeling it creates within. I find it interesting that we humans create such things as movies full of darkness and spend time watching them in order to create a feeling of fear within ourselves. The thrill of watching something, yet knowing we really are not being harmed by it, is almost an addiction, causing our brains to generate dopamine hits that keep us coming back again and again. Yet when we experience something life threatening in real life, we crumble under fear, developing such things as PTSD. Because the body holds energy within it, we begin to cycle that same chemistry of fear through our minds and bodies in a blind effort to resolve it.

Many of us want to avoid anything that causes darkness or fear in our lives—we don't want to be harmed—but we may not realize our own role in creating it. Darkness is generated by an array of emotions and behaviors such as hate, anger, jealousy, envy, lying, racism, oppression, and so on. As you can see, most of our human emotions created from our ego both *come from* some sort of darkness and *contribute to creating it*. When we perpetuate these feelings, beliefs, and emotions, and allow them to influence our behaviors, we develop darkness around us that blocks our ability to love others, be loved, and love ourselves.

The way we develop these parts of our ego are directly related to the programming we receive in the first years of life. As children attempting to find our footing in the world, we are innocently expecting the feelings and qualities of the spirit we so recently emerged from. Our spirit seeks and desires to be, give, and experience love. It does not have darkness within it. But as we are conditioned by the world, we develop darkness which contrasts with what our spirit understands. In this way, the battle between "good and evil" begins, and we spend our lives fighting internally against our spirit and externally against others, trying to resolve it. By placing blame—whether on ourselves through self-hatred, or on something outside of ourselves—we abdicate the power and responsibility we have to compost our own ego and heal what causes the darkness. That is why so many people spend a lifetime seeking something to help them heal, yet never really find it. The clearest example is in religious communities which hold that there is something outside of the self, such as Satan or the devil, along with its many demons, that create the darkness in the world, and that our fight is against these entities rather than our own minds, which create these things in the first place.

As I said, this can be a radical way of thinking and I completely understand if this is clashing up against your ego's understanding of darkness, maybe even causing it to flare up in defense, or fight against this way of seeing the world. But if we take a step back and really look deeply into the reality of what we are, that we are made of love, and in our spirit there is no fault, negative emotions, or discord, then we can see that all the created energies of darkness are simply human made. They are created directly out of and through the ego's programming. I myself went through a period of fighting against this understanding, as my background in religious thinking taught me to believe in the devil and demons. Even in my own experiences I believed I had seen demons or had encounters with them. My ego still at times wants to explain some of the experiences I had as evil entities such as demons, trying to cause me harm or hold me hostage to my emotions. I still remember the first time I came across another church member who shared with me they didn't believe in demons. I was shocked! I thought to myself, how can you not believe in demons with all the evil and darkness in the world? It made no sense to me at the time that there could be something else that created the darkness I was experiencing in my life.

Some of the most interesting experiences I have had in my life involved seeing dark shadows. The first one I ever saw was the one I mentioned in my first book of the dark shadow on my closet door as a small child. This shadow was frightening to me at that young age. I often think about that shadow even now as an adult and try to figure out what, or who it was. I have seen this same figure or something very similar many times throughout my adult life. Because of the fear I had then, and the understanding of the world I had developed in my small mind, it is no wonder that this figure appeared to be evil to me. As we get older our unprogrammed minds we had as children begin to be transformed into the thinking of those around us who are teaching us how to behave and fit in based on the culture we live in. As children we naturally trust this guidance to lead us on the right path, and to truth and understanding of the world around us. In our naive trust, we blindly follow the adults that mold and teach us to become the people we are. Many of us do not remember the beginning years of our life or what molded us into who we are now, nor are we fully aware of other outside influences causing us to have the thinking we do now. Slowly we began to develop a perspective of the world through our ego's lens, and began to behave, think, and act much like those around us.

The more programmed we are, the more separated we feel from our true self. Disconnecting from the spirit, we develop an inner conflict between our ego and spirit, cultivating more and more of an energetic barrier between our conscious and subconscious mind. Any trauma we experience adds even more disconnection from our true self, causing us to experience and see the world around us through a lens of pain, abandonment, fear, or shame, which then informs our behaviors. The programming we develop is directly related to the energies of those around us. We energetically align with them so as to fit in with them, and manifest lifestyles that appear similar. We may even acquire the same type of home, and dress or speak the same way. A child's survival depends on fitting in with their tribe and family, and we fear that if we don't, we will become an outcast. We take this habit into our adult lives. Because we are so influenced by the world around us in this way, we don't notice how we become a part of it.

A good example of this energetic alignment is the way that women's menstruation, after spending time with other women, will change based on the cycles of those around them. We are so energetically connected to others, without even realizing it our bodies begin to manifest the same cycles, energies, and behaviors as those around us. So it makes sense that based on the area you live in, the culture you are in, the beliefs you hold, you find yourself in similar circles and energies that continue to confirm your own beliefs and behaviors.

The void of being disconnected from our spirit, which is where self-love is manifested in its fullest, causes us to seek the love we desire through things or people outside of ourselves.

To heal this, we must first become aware of it. However, even when we do become aware, it can still be difficult to let it go. Like attracts like. Often, we seek out individuals who hold the same energy as we do, hoping they can help us find the deep connection within ourselves. This is a completely unconscious behavior. Disconnected from self, we have no ability to know what the self needs. When we are around people that hold the same kind of programming and energy we hold, we are less likely to see a problem with our own thinking, behaviors, or actions. We need the company of others who do not have the same energy or thinking that we do, to allow us to see ourselves through their eyes. It is also why it is so important to find a healer that has done their own healing, so they are advanced enough to see and point out the areas in which we keep ourselves stuck.

Sometimes when others point out negative behaviors in us without skill, or when we are not connected to self, we feel shame, anger, or any other version of trauma responses of fight, flight, or freeze. We might decide there is something wrong with them, or that they are bad people because we feel criticized. What we must realize in these moments is that they, too, contain toxic energy they hold within themselves, and that energy is what informs them and their behavior. It is all they know to be true for them, it is the best they can do. This is why it is so important to work towards connecting to our true self and developing the ability to love even in moments when we are triggered or when we trigger another. The work of composting the ego is not about ridding ourselves of it completely; rather, it is to train it to respond and react differently in a world that holds so much darkness—the same darkness we are all working to overcome.

For example, if I were to go and purchase a video game with the theme of violence and went to play the game expecting something casual in nature, I would find it to be emotionally triggering. If I then blamed the video game for triggering me because it was not what I was expecting, I would be avoiding responsibility for the fact that I was aware of the violence yet ignored the signs. Becoming upset and defensive about the programming of the video game doesn't change it. The game was created and programmed to be violent, therefore it is performing exactly as it was created to. Expecting it to be or do something different only causes me to become dysregulated and upset because of the conflict within my own self. It was not the video game's doing, it was my own held energy that created a mistaken expectation that caused the frustration and discord within. Similarly, in relationship with ourselves, our perceptions and beliefs about ourselves manifest into our reality and are projected outward onto others around us. Our behaviors, beliefs and actions are driven by what we hold within. The value of having a trigger is that we develop an awareness, and a willingness to rid ourselves of the unwanted behavior and negative mindset. It is only by reprogramming the mind and body that something new can be created. This takes time, effort, and a willingness to do so.

Because this is such a subtle process in the human mind and consciousness, we are usually completely unaware that we are the ones creating dark energy in and around us based on the energy we hold within. Then we wonder why we feel a certain way. But when we become aware of the energy, we have a choice about what we want to do with it. We can either become triggered and place blame on others, or take accountability for the energy we hold, knowing that yes, it may have been caused by something outside of ourselves or an experience we had, but we also have the choice to work toward composting that same darkness into good. We are the creators of our lives and have the power within to be reprogrammed and manifested anew. If we choose not to begin the process of composting this energy, we continue creating more of the same, and this is how the energy of darkness is created and continues to manifest in our lives and in the world around us.

One of the core needs and desires of a human being is connection. Connection is what drives us to be who we are. Because we are energetically made of love, when we lose touch with this part of ourselves, it is natural for our ego to take over and find ways to seek for it outside of the self. When we are children, we develop habits and behaviors to please the adults around us and conform to the other children we spend time with. Many parents that have trauma in their lives, or self-defeating beliefs, unknowingly project those onto the child, and create cycles of manifesting the same struggles within family lines, sometimes for many generations. These are generational karmic cycles. Karma is simply the law of cause and effect over time. In your earthly birth, you are at the effect of causes which create effects in you, which then create new causes that create new effects in subsequent lives. This is how karmic cycles are passed down energetically from the body of the parents to their children, and their children and so on. It makes sense that some of the same struggles a parent had, a child may have at some point in their lives.

The person in the family that becomes aware of the karmic cycles they've been handed has to overcome barriers and conflicts in order to go against the programmed beliefs and stored energy of the family structure. Sometimes they are the scapegoat of the family, yet often they are the ones who begin healing, connecting back to their spirit, which in return causes the frequency they hold to change. When the frequency of a person's energy changes, those around them usually have a very hard time relating to them or understanding them. This can make it hard to understand one another, hear one another, relate to each other, and sadly, at times it causes the relationship to end. As one person's energy shifts, it can be triggering for the other person who has not yet started to heal.

Most people are not aware they are being led by an ego, and therefore have no idea they have the ability to connect with something higher than themselves. Our training by the world is often so good that the reality we manifest in our lives becomes our natural state of being. We feel comfortable behaving within the same programming over and over, never challenging it, or becoming aware that there is another way of doing things. A lot of the stored energies we have in our bodies do form some type of darkness, which becomes the lens we view life from. It is almost as if we are viewing our lives through dense fog. This brings me to one of the reasons why I became so scared of the dark shadows I came in contact with in my life. When we are in our ego, we are unable to fully understand things through our spirit. So, it is natural that a child who is still developing their understanding of the world might see things such as shadows or spirits and become frightened of them, especially depending on what we are told to think about it when we share the experience with an adult.

I do want to note that darkness and demonic spirits are very real to those who experience them. They are scary and can be life altering if experienced over and over with no awareness of how to manage them. Without the ability to know that we can change our thoughts and reprogram our mind (barring mental health disorders or the limitations due to illness in the body) we may never know that we have the ability to stop these experiences simply by reprogramming our thinking. We truly can manifest new experiences in our lives just by thinking differently.

But this requires the tools needed to reprogram our mind. As I mentioned at the beginning of this chapter, I once did not have the tools to manage or fight off negative thoughts, experiences, and energies, so I imagined them as evil, the result of demons or evil spirits. But through diving deep into the healing of the mind, exposing and challenging my beliefs, I was able to begin to manifest new experiences and understand life from a very different perspective. By healing my mind, facing the dark energy I held within myself, I was able to create a connection between my ego and spirit that helped me change my energy and enhance the frequency I brought to the world. Through tools of mindfulness, meditation, awareness of energy and sound, along with coming back into the knowledge of the true self hidden within the walls of the ego, we are able to compost the dark energy into light, and begin to break away from cycles, experiences, and the energy of darkness, frequency by frequency.

Chapter 7

Balance

An old grandfather was teaching his grandson about life:

"A fight is going on inside me," he said to the boy.

"It is a terrible fight and it is between two wolves. One is evil—he is anger, envy, sorrow, regret, greed,

*arrogance, self-pity, guilt,
resentment, inferiority, lies, false
pride, superiority, and ego."*

*He continued, "The other is good—
he is joy, peace, love, hope, serenity,
humility, kindness, empathy,
generosity, truth, compassion, and
faith. The same fight is going on
inside you—and inside every other
person, too."*

*The grandson thought about it for a
minute and then asked his
grandfather: "Which wolf will win?"*

*The grandfather simply replied, "The
one you feed."*

This is a popular story of unknown origins, and
this is the most common way it ends. However,

there are other versions, and one I like ends like
this:

> *The grandson thinks about this for a*
> *few minutes, and then asks his*
> *grandfather, "Which wolf wins?"*

> *The grandfather replies, "They both*
> *win if you feed them right."*

> *"You see, if I starve one wolf, the*
> *other will become imbalanced with*
> *power. If I choose to feed only the*
> *light wolf, for example, the shadow*
> *one will become ravenous and*
> *resentful. He will hide around every*
> *corner and wait for my defenses to*
> *lower, then attack. He will be filled*
> *with hatred and jealousy and will*
> *fight the light wolf endlessly.*

"But if I feed both, in the right way, at the right time, they will live side-by-side in harmony. There will be no more inner battle. Instead, there will be inner peace. And when there's peace, there is wisdom. The goal of life, my child, is to respect this balance of life, for when you live in balance, you can serve the Great Spirit within. When you put an end to the battle inside, you are free."

In this version, the grandfather has a deep understanding of both his spirit and ego, how each works alongside the other, but also separately; both have a role to play. Because one part does not exist without the other, he encourages the grandson to learn to balance them.

In the tarot deck you will find several cards that represent balance, one of which is the *Temperance* card. *Temperance* is one of the *Major Arcana*—22 of the 78 cards of the tarot that represent the large archetypal themes we all face in the grand scheme of life. On the *Temperance* card, there is an androgynous angel with wings, suggesting a balance between masculine and feminine energy. One foot of the angel is in water, symbolic of the subconscious, while the other foot is on dry land, a representation of the material world, or the conscious mind. On the angel's robe is a square with a triangle inscribed inside—a symbol of the tangible earth in union with the holy trinity. She holds two cups which also represent the conscious and subconscious minds. Water flows between them, seemingly in both directions, suggesting union and infinity. Everything about this card represents balance, the perfect harmony that comes from the union of dualities. The ego composting into the spirit.

Most of us are not aware that our projection of the world is based on our own judgments about ourselves. As we have already learned, the assumptions we've developed about the world around us and how we should live come from how we are raised and our cultural background. It is hard to see past these beliefs and views when they are the water we swim in.

Throughout history humans have developed hierarchical systems, exercising domination and control over one another, creating an imbalance of masculine energy over the feminine. Many political beliefs, religious teachings, and leadership qualities were developed from the assumption that masculine energies are superior to and should dominate feminine energies. This paradigm assumes that one person is always above or below another based on a person's beliefs or status, and pits people against one another. With the excessive cultivation of this mindset, vulnerability has been lost and the deeper connection with each other has become harder to develop. We all seek connection and love, as this is what our spirits desire and are made from. But due to being detached from our spirit, humans seek validation and love through the ego self. Our workplaces, friendships, romantic relationships, and even family units, are pervaded by this atmosphere of imbalance. This imbalance prevents humans from seeing one another as their true selves and creates barriers to vulnerability and love. The lack of connection between humans adds another layer of trauma to the ego self, and a repetitive cycle is created of disconnect and imbalance. In order for this cycle to be broken it needs to be first acknowledged and then seen through the eyes of the spirit self.

On an individual level we can create a lifestyle so busy, we barely have time to sit, contemplate, and connect with our spirit. It can be challenging to create time to just be, and to reflect on the positive aspects of who we are outside of our "doing." The constant "doing" gives the impression that our life is full and of value, and we can be so consumed with constantly striving and working hard, we begin to believe that our worth only comes through doing. By filling our time with activities we think give us worth, we begin to present a polished outward ego to the world that encases us, keeping us separated from others and even from ourselves. Trapped in these walls, the spirit is unable to manifest its qualities into the world. In our constant striving, we perpetuate the imbalance of masculine energy over feminine energy.

It is instructive to observe what happens when a society is forced by circumstance to be vulnerable, the walls between people broken down, such as after a natural disaster. However, even with collective hardship and grief there is still an aspect of performance and drive to move through it quickly, to get "back to normal," to cover over the exposure of our vulnerability and need for connection. We plunge back into the cycle of performance and separation. It is almost as if these events are trying to teach us to be more vulnerable and connected, yet we have a hard time allowing them to reshape our world, to sustain the opening.

In an age where social media influences how we view the world, we can find ourselves trapped in a continual loop of propping up our egos, perpetually comparing ourselves to others and trying to control our image and how we are perceived. We may believe the person next to us has something figured out that we do not, or vice versa, we think we are better than another. Both views come from the ego-self. When the ego is untamed, it is constantly comparing or controlling, attempting to cover over or decrease the negative feelings we have of ourselves, but producing more and more negativity in the process. Much like the evil wolf, it is full of envy, jealousy, false pride, and resentment, fabricating stories and collecting evidence to justify itself. All along we have no idea that we are manifesting the lives we have based on the thoughts we have.

When I became serious about my spiritual practices, I noticed the narrative in my mind was changing. Things I once saw as purely negative

I began to see as the universe guiding me on my path. Slowly, the realization dawned that I had spent most of my life working on the outward and not connecting inward, and I realized it was my thoughts that needed to change. All my life I thought I should pray to a God outside myself, and would often do so, but I was never fully connected with the God consciousness inside of myself. I was not loving myself by my actions, words, or thoughts. Instead, I was focused on changing my outside appearance in order to manage how others saw me, which did nothing to improve how I saw myself. The energy I spent manipulating and changing myself to get validation from outside only produced spirals of shame and self-hatred, requiring my ego to become even more self-focused. I drank, isolated myself, was defensive, starved my body, and overextended myself through exercise and hard work in attempts to regain my sense of worth, to no avail. I was stuck in cycles of behavior that perpetuated my misery, which I desperately wanted to escape, when all along, it was thoughts I had towards myself I needed to work on.

Meditation allows the mind to refocus and bring a balance between the outside and the inside. It brings awareness to the spirit self, allowing it to work alongside the ego, transforming thought, behavior, and beliefs. Becoming more mindful in your life allows a release of anxieties that undermine the life you truly desire. Instead of focusing on the anxieties of yesterday or tomorrow, we bring awareness to the very moment we are in, releasing the knots of energy holding us back from our subconsciousness. Once we are connected with our subconsciousness, we align with our higher self.

Much like what the grandfather was teaching his grandson, we can reprogram the mind by focusing on the calming stillness on the inside, allowing the subconscious mind to come alongside the ego mind. This process creates a balancing of energies. The spirit is gentle and flowing, while the ego can be a bit more forceful and demanding. However, both the spirit and ego have qualities that serve our higher purpose. Most would likely say that the ego is more masculine and the spirit feminine. Source, which we call God, is both masculine and feminine, completely united and working in harmony. The only separation we could consider God to have is in us, in the discord between ego and spirit. But since we are also God's energy, we are God experiencing itself, through our human form, seeking alignment in our daily lives—not separated from God, but one.

Before and into the 14th century it was considered masculine for a man to wear garments that resembled what today we would call a dress. For an extremely long time, the tunic or short skirt was a key part of the male outfit. Slowly, beliefs about masculine energy, and perspectives on what made a "man" shifted, which led to skirts becoming less and less acceptable for males. By the 20th century this style of dress for men had been eliminated, reflecting cultural expectations that men eschew their feminine qualities altogether. All progress in the 20th century was considered to the work of men, an expression of masculine qualities such as rationality and ambition; relegated to second-class citizenship, women fought successfully to be seen as equal to men, but this did not change the belief that the masculine energy was superior to feminine energies. There remains an imbalance in the world between these qualities, the harmony of which makes each of us more like God. Returning to our divine nature requires bringing the two back into their balanced power. In some ways society is acknowledging the value of feminine traits even in men, but there is a long way to go. I am unsure if there was ever a true balance of these energies on the earth, but to truly come back into Christ-like consciousness, this balance is necessary.

In the vision in which I experienced God's energy and love and saw spirits being created through it, God was not a male or female. There was not a sex involved in this image, it was just a divine being of light energy. Valuing male qualities above female ones, humans began addressing God as "he" instead of "she" or even "it," unable to see the two as one. The way the Bible was written also refers to God as "he." We, being made in the image of God, choose to come to earth in a body with a certain sex. In my religious mindset I often wondered about those who do not resonate with the sex of their body. Being able to grasp the concept that there is no true sex in the spirit allowed my mind to relax some and release the grip on needing to label others based solely on the body we are in. Sex is a biological need for the sake of human procreation, and it can also be a source of bonding and pleasure. If you were to study animals, however, you would learn that some of them can reproduce asexually, while others can switch sexes depending on environmental factors. This is a beautiful example of how life itself is made of both male and female energies and that there are many ways of expressing that unity.

The ego's need to perform or conform is often a barrier to living our lives authentic to ourselves.

We are continually abandoning ourselves to please others around us out of fear of disappointing others or being rejected. Because our self-esteem depends on the acceptance we receive from others rather than from within, we focus more on what others think about us than on what we actually need. Feelings of being unlovable or unkind keep us in repeated cycles of putting others before our own needs and adds to the disconnection we are already facing within ourselves. Those that are learning to trust themselves, to make positive decisions free from the compulsion to please others, understand that the body does not always reflect what a person's true nature is. Feelings that arise within the body based in fear are not the true feelings of our higher self, but of the ego self. Each person is on their own separate journey, creating and learning from the lessons created through their ego. The more we connect with our true self, balancing our spirit and ego with inner love, the more open we become to allowing others to have their own experience without needing to abandon our own authentic experience at the same time—we can accept our differences. Living our life aligned with spirit requires the continual composting of parts of ourselves that keep us stuck in negative thinking towards ourselves or others. It allows us to see others as their higher self just as we are working to do for ourselves. When we are able to do this, we calm the fear in the ego, knowing that we can take care of our needs, and the other will be okay because they, too, have a higher self they can connect with to be fulfilled from within.

In the process of composting the old patterns in our lives, it can feel as if our entire system is being moved and shifted into places we have never been before, which can feel quite uncomfortable. The physical body may react with feelings of anxiety, confusion, shame, and fear. It's almost like an earthquake happens within our bodies. The work of balancing the ego and spirit shifts our energy, and destabilizes the foundations upon which we once built our understanding of ourselves and the world. We must learn to build a new foundation of understanding in order to find our balance again. As we find our balance, our perspective begins to change, and we develop a different way of being and thinking in the world. This not only shakes our own foundation, but can be disturbing for others around us who have become accustomed to us as we were. What we must remember is that under the surface of our awareness, in the body and in the subconscious, energy and emotions from previous experiences have been stored way, never properly digested. As we shift and shake them out, they move to the surface to be felt, maybe for the first time in our lives. Acknowledging these uncomfortable feelings opens us up to a higher perspective and connection with our true selves.

We have a choice when they arise to either allow them to shake out of us (feeling them fully and letting them go), or to store them back into the body, remaining the same. If we allow the process, it will transform us. From the inside outward, we begin to change our way of showing up in the world. While others may remain in the same place, our foundation has been moved, and this movement creates seismic shifts in which we become more connected to our highest self and release what is not aligned. The shifting is a lifelong process and there is always something to release or move. But the more you engage in the process, the easier and quicker you become aware when your body is attempting to shift something out of it, and likely will even welcome the experience, knowing that it is helping you become your highest self.

Our higher self, spirit, guides, angels, are always communicating with us, but without the alignment and balancing in our own energy to receive the messages, we are unable to hear them. When we limit ourselves to what we have been taught by other humans, and do not spend the time to go inward and connect with our intuition, we are missing a part of the human experience that allows us to manifest into reality the life we truly desire. Other humans can help in the process of learning these tools and aligning ourselves back with our highest self, but it takes building an authentic relationship with our own selves, learning to trust our own energy and intuition, to truly balance our energy and

learn how to live aligned with our highest self—
not discarding the ego (which isn't possible) but
putting it in its proper place within our life.

Chapter 8:

Be Still

If you follow teachings on manifesting, you will have learned about the law of attraction, and raising your vibration to meet the level of the desires you want to manifest. When I consider this way of teaching I often think about the vision of the leaf, and the rocks that we find ourselves stuck behind. As I began my journey of learning more about the importance of releasing and flowing, and as I continued my healing journey, I would notice my energy was changing as well. The old beliefs and limiting thoughts would still pop up once in a while, but no longer were causing me to be stuck. By noticing them, allowing myself to experience and feel the emotions associated with them, and then releasing them, I was able to stay in the flow of moving forward in my life. Because we are such habitual creatures and our mind causes many obstacles in our lives, making these changes often seems more difficult than it really is.

Leaving behind the rules we've been conditioned to live by in society, and the beliefs we developed throughout our lives, is scary. We may worry about what others think of us as we make changes, fearing the judgment we've internalized in the back of our minds, and hold ourselves back from doing the things we desire.

However, those desires deep within us that continue to surface throughout our lives, prodding at our heart, will never disappear. Those proddings are of our spirit pushing us towards our purpose. When someone begins to respond to those inner promptings, it can cause others to take stock and reflect on themselves. If they experience this as in conflict with the way they have always behaved or what they've always believed, it can cause irritation, fear, or jealousy.

The ego feels threatened by others who escape the confines of egoic programming, so people in our lives may begin to project their own internal fears onto us. Not only do we have the obstacle of overcoming our own limiting beliefs and mindset, but also the limiting beliefs of others. This is where many become stuck. However, it is important to understand that the obstacles themselves create the necessity to go inward, to take refuge with our true selves, to heal and transform the areas that keep us stuck. Whether it be fear, stored traumas, limiting beliefs, or the projections of others, the discomfort we experience is like the irritant that causes an oyster to produce a beautiful pearl. Without these experiences the stored energies are never challenged to change. The process can be so uncomfortable, that many people choose not to engage it at all.

The potential to grow and change is within each and every one of us. To access this change we must shed parts of our ego that keeps us stuck in old, programmed beliefs and behaviors. In order to do this, we must become quiet enough to discover ourselves on a deeper level, revealing parts of the ego that need to be shed, and what parts will benefit our journey. Spending most of our lives unaware of ourselves at this level, it seems to be a daunting task to begin the journey of going within. But learning to be still and quiet is indispensable. Doing so, we teach our ego how to pause and allow space for the spirit to speak to us. As Jesus in the Bible calms the storm, we must calm the storm within. The ego causes an internal squall, loud and demanding, and our emotions take precedence over the still and gentle guidance of our spirit.

In stillness, going inward, we begin to develop the ability to hear the deep inner knowing of our spirit. The ego desires to rush and control, the mind never calm enough to be still. That is why the daily practice of meditation and training the mind to become still over and over is the key to bringing balance between the ego and spirit. The ego, by its very nature, will fight against the process. Our ego's job is to keep us safe, doing whatever we need to do to survive. Being still doesn't seem to serve a purpose in this regard. Panic arises within the ego, urging us not to waste our time being still and quiet. Our mind is used to the neurochemical rewards generated by being on task and performance. Becoming still causes an uncomfortable conflict in our body, maybe even causing us to avoid the quiet all together. We are programmed to believe that growth only comes through hard work and even sometimes tears—we struggle to trust that simply becoming quiet is enough to help us move forward in life. The practice of meditation is training our ego that it is safe to be calm, to release the resistance, and to flow with the natural state of the spirit. We discover it is only our programming that is keeping us stuck in repeated cycles in our lives, that causes burnout and stress, disconnection from self, and a continual struggle of moving forward.

That programming, our ego, is designed to protect us from pain and harm. Since healing may uncover pain, the ego avoids it at all costs. I have had clients who say they fear allowing themselves to feel the pain of going within, they worry that once the emotions are exposed, they may never go away. The idea of letting the stored pain inside be expressed outward also means that they may no longer be the person they believe they are. Because pain is stored in our body as energy, and the energy is connected to our ego, the mind associates the pain with the person's identity, clinging to it in spite of the suffering it causes. Those who take this journey of going inward, releasing the pain, and working to decrease self-limiting thoughts, are some of the most courageous people in the world. It is not an easy task to become still with ourselves.

Fear is one of the main reasons we become stuck in our lives. Allowing our feelings to control us hinders our ability to manifest the lives we truly desire. If we don't take the time to be aware of what the source of these emotions is, we push them back down inside the body, hold them in our minds, and continue to manifest more of the same energy in our lives. When we only focus outward to understand our suffering, the circumstances that happen often feel even more devastating than they actually are. Keeping our focus on outward circumstances perpetuates the inner battle between the ego and spirit. If we never allow ourselves to become still enough to be aware of this inner battle, it will last a lifetime.

The body keeps track of each event experienced in our lives (like notes in an outline for a story), It does this to keep track of patterns that the animal (or person) can use to help navigate the dangers of life. For example, if a baby deer witnesses another deer killed by a predator, all the things associated with that experience will be imprinted in the deer's body so they can recognize the danger earlier next time it comes around and hopefully escape.

Human beings are more complicated than other animals, however, and this mechanism can actually backfire. Our mind creates a story based on that saved material, which becomes the narrative of our life. If there is a narrative based on fear stored in the body, fear is what will be manifested through behaviors. These behaviors and their results then appear to substantiate the narrative—fear begets more things to fear, aggression begets more to fight against, a victim-stance creates more of a sense of powerlessness and so on. When more of the same energy shows up in our lives, we fortify our story, and make it our identity. We continually look for evidence to feed the ego, the identity which in the name of self-protection actually keeps us disconnected from our spirit.

For example, if we grew up feeling unlovable, a "note" was written based on this feeling, and stored in our bodies. "Need to do xyz to gain love and be protected." If we don't take the time to go inward and notice this note, see it is no longer relevant and discard or rewrite it, that energy will influence us to do "xyz" over and over again, no matter how detrimental the results. The energy within will seek justification in attempts to finally be effective—generating the same energy again and again.

The opposite is also true. If we have a "note" stored in our body based on experiencing agency and success in overcoming obstacles, we will not be put off by obstacles and will keep looking for the solutions to move forward. It all comes down to the subconscious mind and our thoughts. The mind has the power to convince us we are stuck no matter what, or that we can succeed if we keep trying. The stories we tell ourselves, and the energy we store in our bodies, whether negative or positive, influence how we think and behave, which in turn has an effect on what happens. This is why it is so important to become still and know what energy we hold within.

It is possible in some cases, if the stored energy is too deeply ingrained in someone's body, it can cause a complete disconnection between the ego and spirit. That person may become so engulfed in the negative energies of their narrative, that they develop pathological behaviors such as narcissism. With no self-awareness or connection to the spirit within, the unbalanced ego creates a block too strong to overcome. In such cases, the ego has such control over the person's mind, it is almost impossible for the spirit's gentle voice to get through. The ability to reconnect with their spirit is severely inhibited as it has been choked out of their lives. It is best to allow such people to go through their own process, to set healthy boundaries with them, and allow them to work through it in their own time. The truth remains that we are eternal beings, so when these people return to their true nature after the death of the body, they will then have a chance to come to terms with the energy they held during that lifetime.

For those who have not been disconnected from the spirit fully, there is always hope of a reconnection. There may be an energetic density and fog to look through, but it is possible to do the inner work by becoming still, learning to calm the ego mind, and quiet the many storms it can create. Once the storm begins to settle, the fog begins to clear, and the light can become bright enough to see the areas that need to be deconstructed and released. Going through this process of healing, growing, and reconnecting with our highest self, we develop empathy and compassion, not only for those around us, but for ourselves as we learn how to heal the story written within. It becomes easier to love others as we learn how to love ourselves. We can see that others are fighting the same inner demons and barriers that we are. Though there can still be conflicts that arise due to our ego (as this part never fully disappears), we become much more aware and skilled at bringing compassion to others, instead of judgment.

You may have heard the idea that everyone around you is a mirror of yourself. This is true because we attract circumstances and relationships that reflect our personal narrative— we magnetize energies that resonate with the energy we hold inside. We tend to be surrounded by others with the same values and beliefs as our own. As you continue to heal and release the old story, you become aware of these patterns in your life, noticing the energetic lines that give shape to the life you are living. It is then, by becoming still enough to hear that quiet inner voice, that we can find the courage to move out of those limited patterns.

Our spirit's energy is at a higher frequency than that of the ego. This can create discord between the two energies. If one person has been taking the time to work on themselves, another who has not started this process might feel uncomfortable around them, struggling to understand the higher frequency. They might even feel threatened as they are still viewing life through the old, programmed story they hold within. The higher frequency is irritating to their inner demons. For those who are healing, it is important to realize that debating with someone or trying to convince them of what we are discovering is useless because each person is fighting their own unique inner battle. Change is intimidating, and the ego will resist it. The best approach is one of compassion and love, allowing others the freedom to go through their own process of healing and connecting with spirit. Our fight is not against flesh and blood, but the inner darkness we each hold within.

When we leave these human bodies we will return to the ease and flow of our true nature. Our human incarnation is a choice to experience the resistance to this flow as a way to come into relationship with the energy we have arisen from. In many ways, we are the universe expanding itself, evolving and growing in frequency. The energy of the universe, or God, is expressing itself, and experiencing itself within each of us. Each human holds a different frequency and experiences life from that unique frequency. That is why the body you live in is so very special and deserves the time taken to treat it well. As we reconnect our spirit and ego, as we release the blocks in our lives, we begin to participate in the flow of energy, attracting and manifesting the potential within our human life.

I am sure many of my readers will have been in a pool when everyone decides it would be fun to start a whirlpool. At first it is fun as everyone goes around the same direction, building up a cyclone-like system in the water. Before you know it, the current becomes too hard to fight against and carries everyone along like it or not. If you are relaxed and welcome this flow, you can enjoy the experience. If you are not one who welcomes the flow, you will find yourself upset and fighting against it, feeling chaotic and out of control. Eventually, once everyone stops the movement, everything calms, and you are able to gain your individual bearings again. This is a nice analogy for our lives. Without even knowing it, we forget to flow with the natural abundance of the spirit, and we find ourselves fighting against the current of our life. We end up trying to force things to work instead of just allowing them to flow. The fight against the current often leaves us exhausted and frustrated. But if we listen to our intuition, become still, and go with the flow, eventually the flow becomes calmer. Then we develop the ability to see more clearly, becoming grounded once again. Releasing the grip of our ego and going with the flow is not easy because the ego is programmed to fight against things it is unfamiliar with. But by creating a connection with our spirit, becoming inwardly still and connecting with its guidance, we release the ego's hold over our lives, and begin to flow with the natural course meant for us.

Chapter 9

Under the Surface

Our dreams carry messages for us if we pay attention to them. If you have a dream that remains vivid the next morning, it probably contains some clues about what is going on in your life. Our intuition is less hindered by the ego mind when we are asleep because we are shutting down our ego's need to perform tasks and maintain awareness of the outside world. Once we release the ego's control and tap into the subconscious, we hear more clearly from our spirit. That's why many people get visions or intuitive messages when sleeping, or right before fully waking.

Scientists have measured five main brainwave frequencies in humans: Beta, Alpha, Theta, Delta, and Gamma. As long as the brain is alive, it is always producing electro-magnetic waves based on its level of activity and state—whether alert and focused on a task, calmly present, or deeply asleep. The theta state of mind happens most often just as we are falling asleep, right before we wake, or in a deep meditative state. It often involves dreams or vivid images, intuitions, and information not usually accessible to our conscious mind. The theta state is used in hypnosis, slowing down the brain, turning attention away from the outer senses, and tapping into the subconscious mind that is usually drowned out by the activities of everyday life. People who meditate often or for many hours at a time are able to achieve this state of complete calmness in both the mind and body. That is why meditation is one of the best practices to allow the spirit to take more of a lead in our lives.

Some of the dreams we have can convey our soul purpose, what we are meant to do during our lifetime on earth. Our subconscious connects us to our spirit, which holds our deepest truths within it. In my dreams I have had insights about my calling in life, or what the next step was for me. At other times I've received messages about unconscious areas in my life I had yet to heal. A dream once gave me a message I didn't understand until over a week later in meditation. In this dream I was walking up to someone's home on a dirt path along a wooden fence. Tall grass and wildflowers were as high as my waste and it was a beautiful setting. As I walked up to the house, I became nervous and decided to hide. Like a child would do, I lay down on the ground, scrunched up into a ball in the tall grass, and placed my feet up on the fence beside me. As I did, I looked up and noticed that a small splinter of wood was sticking out from a post. On top of this splintered wood was a tiny head, almost like a pencil eraser. The head was spinning around on top of the splintered piece of wood. It was eerie and I became anxious as I watched it. Then I noticed a note stapled to the post right above it. I looked at the note and it said, "It will be okay." This gave me peace, and I began to feel more relaxed.

The dream went on with many other messages in it, but what came to me during my meditation was that the tiny head represented my thoughts—spinning, uncontrolled, anxious, worried, confused, and doubting—toxic thoughts that were keeping me stuck in a limiting mindset. The note above it saying "It will be okay" was reminding me that I could release the thoughts and energies I was holding onto; that by connecting back into my intuition, releasing the ego's control, I would be able to bring balance back into my life and continue moving forward in the process of healing and manifesting the life I was meant to live. By taking the focus off the spinning of the head, erasing the thoughts that kept my mind in constant turmoil, I would be able to rest my mind, trust that I'd be okay, and connect back in with my truth. The significance of the note being just above the spinning head was that it's where our crown chakra is located. The crown chakra is the energy center of our body that is responsible for thought, awareness, wisdom, and connection with source energy, God. This chakra regulates the energy of consciousness. There was no doubt this dream was speaking of the many thoughts I held in my mind, keeping me in fear and disconnecting me from my truth. It was reminding me to release the negative, chaotic energy cycling in my mind and trust the divine energy of my spirit.

The second thing that stuck out to me about this dream was how I hid like a child. This was my ego causing me to stay small and hide my authentic self. I reverted into a childlike state when I became anxious and allowed my mind to keep me from moving forward to where I was heading. When we are on a journey of self-discovery it can be intimidating to share our true selves with others when we've kept them hidden for so long. To those who have known us in a different light, it can seem like we've become a different person than who we were prior to the healing. It takes courage to fully show up as our authentic self in all settings; to come out of hiding, letting down the protective walls built up from past experiences. Even though the ego's protection is meant to be useful, it becomes a hindrance preventing us from living as our highest self. If we never come out of hiding, we never move forward in who we are capable of becoming.

Scientists say that we ordinarily use only about 10% of our brains' capabilities. We have the capacity to use more, but the brain functions much like the spinning head in my dream—the 10% is just recycling over and over, limiting our ability to think beyond what has helped us survive so far. That 10% is like the top of an iceberg—if we could look below the water, we would see the magnitude of what we actually have available to us through the subconscious. Without awareness of and practice connecting to the subconscious, we only see the surface level of what is.

This limited view that keeps us from moving forward in life was created in our childhood. When the brain was still developing and events happened that caused discord within, the brain sent warning signals to the body developing strategies for surviving that remain with us as we grow older. Those strategies become walls of protection in our lives that we continue to bump up against when we feel triggered, vulnerable, or exposed. Once protective, these walls now keep us trapped in a story of who we are, which is no longer connected to our truth. But we have the potential to discover that the walls are simply doors we can open if we choose. We are the authors of our lives, and we hold the keys to open any doors preventing us from living our highest truth. Once we realize that every block we face in our lives is actually a door, we have a choice to either stay behind it or go through it.

Instead of looking at obstacles as permanent barriers in our lives, we can retrain our brains to understand them as doors in our thinking that we can open if we are determined. Each door has the potential to provide us with the self-growth and healing we desire if allowed. Our bodies are amazing at communicating with us what is going on below the surface. Much of the energy we hold in our bodies is directly related to our thoughts. The body will give us indications of how we are stuck, but if we continually ignore its messages, it will develop even bigger warning signs such as sickness or turmoil in our lives. Until the body is able to get our attention through these events, it will continue to manifest more and more of the same energy. Many people never take the time to listen to the body's warning signals until developing life altering circumstances that force change. Until we realize that we are the one holding the keys to unlock the doors holding us back in our lives, we will never discover what is behind them.

Deep within each of us is a voice calling for something more. Many of us limit that calling because of fear. Those who fight through the fear and self-doubts and build a community of supportive people and positive energy around them, are able to move forward and inspire others to heal as well. You can't force things to grow. You can't force healing. You can't rush the process of connecting with your highest self. Releasing behaviors and beliefs requires stillness and patience. Many go through life assuming what we see on the surface level of life is accurate and true. But when we take the time to look beneath the surface, we finally begin to notice the areas of our lives that keep our heads spinning, our minds in fear, and our focus on the barriers in our lives. Composting these areas of the ego that no longer serve our highest good brings us to the understanding that our true self is the spirit. Just one person making the choice to open the closed doors in their lives empowers others to do so in their lives as well. Diving deep under the ego and connecting with our truth not only benefits our lives but the many others around us that are inspired to dive into their own process of composting the ego as well.

Chapter 10

Repeated Messages

I realize there are repeated phrases circulating in my books, and you may read similar messages and guidance in other authors' books relating to spiritual growth or healing. One of the hardest things for the ego to let go of is the belief that we already know it all; this shuts us down from hearing a message again, or in a new way. If you have made it this far in the book, you've begun the work of overcoming that barrier. There is a saying, "The best teachers are also the best students." Those who don't need to always be right or think everything they believe in the moment is completely true, are the ones that grow in knowledge and are more likely to continue expanding into their highest self. They are also more likely to remain humble as they are aware that there is always more to learn, more to grow in, and more unlearning in the processes of connecting with their highest self.

The spirit repeats itself and the message it shares because we may not always hear it accurately the first time. Or if we hear it accurately, maybe we haven't applied it to our lives. Just like it takes a regular practice of meditation to calm the mind, we often need to continue learning the same lessons over and over until we fully benefit from them. Sometimes the fear that arises in the ego is masked by a know-it-all mentality. Whether we realize it or not, this attitude actually manifests more fear and disconnection between the subconscious and conscious. Each time we reject a message or twist it in our ego mind to fit what we already understand, it enhances the resistance. The belief that it is already all known, and that there is nothing more to learn, is just another impediment between our spirit and ego.

Since many of the messages we get in spirit are of a higher frequency than what our minds hold, we can reject the message altogether or try to make it fit our current belief system. The rational mind is not equipped to comprehend the messages of the spirit on its own; it is only through alignment with the highest self that we even begin to understand because our intuition starts to grow. As we heal, learn, apply new skills to our lives, and enhance the frequency of our energy, we hear the messages more clearly, or in a different way, and can benefit from them. Those who have spent many years meditating often share about times during the meditation when the mind is able to finally let go. Almost every single one of these people will mention that the ego mind tries to co-opt these moments as an excitement comes over them and the mind begins to think it finally has reached its goal. Letting even that idea go, deep meditation takes over from the mind, and in this space we are fully able to hear from the spirit and reach a moment of true enlightenment. Once in a while, those of us who meditate are able to stay in that frequency a bit longer, sometimes receiving messages that can change the direction of our lives or the lives of others we share it with. I believe that everyone has the ability to do this. It just takes time to train our mind to let go its resistance, releasing the ramblings of the spinning mind, and connecting deep within to the true self, our spirit. Through inner work, we all can reconnect with our truth, and even the truth of the world around us.

Because the human mind is easily programmed in the first years of a child's life, the beliefs and behaviors of a person have been held for a lifetime. Until we begin the process of reconnecting with our spirit, we are completely unaware of the nature of this training and programming; it is so embedded in our minds, we just assume we were born to behave and believe as we are. But none of us were born programmed to behave the way we do now as adults. We were taught this by our parents or caregivers, and our parents were taught by theirs. Think about this. If we had been raised by a gorilla, we would grow up behaving and thinking as a gorilla, not knowing the difference. I think Disney was onto something when they created the movie Tarzan. This is a great representation of how culture and society program us to behave and think.

If you think about a baby's first days on this earth, much of the time the parents are spending with the baby is in an attempt to get it to stop behaving as it is—to get the baby to stop crying, they feed it, rock it, hold it, or even at times, leave it alone to cry it out hoping eventually it will stop. Some of this training is healthy and needed for a child. It would be a strange world and very funny, if we all walked around crying and screaming whenever we wanted or needed something. Yet again, if that was how it was, none of us would think it was strange. We would just cry and scream right along with everyone else. Until one day, someone finally realizes that the way of behaving was simply not working, and there had to be a better way of getting our needs met. If that person began to change and behave differently, there would be others who would fight the idea of changing the way they have always done things and continue to cry and scream. So, the training of a baby is necessary, it just has the potential to close us off from the spirit as it becomes more about performing for others than becoming our fullest selves.

Take a step back for a moment in your mind and consider the world as a whole. Maybe visualize yourself up in the universe looking down. Let yourself imagine the many different cultures there are all around the earth; the variety of languages spoken, the colors of skin, the religious beliefs, and all the ways of thinking.

Composting the Ego

Each of these cultures has their own energy frequency as well. The energy of each culture is connected throughout the earth, connecting all humans as one. One person on one side of the earth and another on the other side may hold the same frequency of understanding of the world, yet still be very different based on their programming. No two humans see the same things, hear the same things, or learn in the same way. There are many similarities, even universalities, but a multitude of different perspectives. It can be hard to wrap the ego mind around the idea of energy and frequency being what connects the human race, yet also separates them. The more work one does to compost the ego, connecting back into the true self, and aligning with spirit, the more the eyes of the ego become enlightened and aware, transparent to a different frequency. In spiritual terms this awareness is often called our "third eye."

One of the inherent tendencies of the ego mind is to compare and categorize in its attempt to make sense of the world. This gives rise to fears and insecurities because of the many differences between people. Judgment and criticism become our constant companions, trying to sort the "good" from the "bad." The ego sees things in overly simplistic terms—the way I am doing something is right and the other person has it wrong (or vice versa) and this causes conflict between individuals and groups, which then creates more of the dark energy we are all fighting against and wanting to release from our lives. Or we try to align ourselves to others, to go along and fit in, even going against our own nature in attempts to be loved, accepted, and have connection. Yet the true connection we seek is the connection with self. Until we understand this, we will continue seeking something outside ourselves to fill the void within that only we can fill.

We judge ourselves against others without even realizing that they, too, were trained to be as they are. But many who have embraced the healing journey, connecting back with the higher self, begin to understand this and see how those around them are only able to comprehend their reality based on the frequency they hold within. This understanding cultivates empathy and compassion, and allows room for each individual human to be where they are without the need to change them or pressure them to believe, become, or act like anyone else around them.

Another trigger for the ego is when we create something or speak something that we believe is original to us, and then see someone else doing the same. If our ego is untrained, we don't realize that a message from the spirit is shared in many different frequencies and forms and through many people; the ego can feel threatened at the thought of not receiving credit and attention for what it considers its own unique revelation.

I have found myself in my own ego mind believing I know everything there is to know about a subject and feeling fear that someone would get the attention I believed I should have. All of this comes from the insecurities of the ego, which doesn't understand there truly is nothing new under the sun, and even our original thoughts and ideas are likely recycled energies that have been understood or taught before. Going even deeper into this understanding, even what we think of as original is not truly original because everything comes from the one source, a frequency of energy generating all creation.

Vanity of vanities," says the Preacher; "Vanity of vanities, all is vanity." What does man gain from all his labor in which he labors under the sun?

One generation goes, and another generation comes; but the earth remains forever. The sun also rises, and the sun goes down, and hurries to its place where it rises.

The wind goes toward the south, and turns around to the north. It turns around continually as it goes, and the wind returns again to its courses.

All the rivers run into the sea, yet the sea is not full. To the place where the rivers flow, there they flow again.

All things are full of weariness beyond uttering. The eye is not satisfied with seeing, nor the ear filled with hearing.

That which has been is that which shall be, and that which has been done is that which shall be done; and there is no new thing under the sun. Is there a thing of which it may be said, "Behold, this is new?"

It has been long ago, in the ages which were before us. There is no memory of the former; neither shall there be any memory of the latter that are to come, among those that shall come after.

The World English Bible; Ecclesiastes 1:1-11

The speaker is King Solomon, who describes his own awakening process, realigning with spirit and developing an understanding of God's true energy. Everything on earth is continually composting and fleeting, nothing lasting, always an ebb and flow. This ebb and flow is why the spirit self-decided to manifest through earth to experience human life. It is somewhat incomprehensible but the reality is that we choose to live a human life in order to experience the disruption and blocks of the ego. It is only in this lower frequency that our spirit can learn and grow. In the higher realms and frequency of heaven, there is nothing to learn or grow from, all is aligned and complete. So in many ways, our ego mind is helping the spirit to grow and expand in its frequency. Maybe those who have developed this connection between the ego and spirit in this lifetime are the ones who have lived many lives before and have developed an ability to attune back into the higher self and its frequency more quickly.

Given that there is nothing new under the sun, even the most profound teachings will be repeated in different ways at different time so everyone will hear. Each human embodies their own frequency in the world. Therefore, what one person writes or speaks will not vibrate at the same frequency that everyone can hear and comprehend. Some messages may have to be shared at lower frequencies while others higher. Because there are so many layers of energy and frequencies on the earth, not everyone will hear at the same level. Messages from the spirit will change form based on the frequency of both the speaker and audience. Jesus often chose to teach through parables, as they were easier for his listeners to understand. The many different forms of the same message being shared by different teachers are the spirit's attempt to reach many different types of people based on their current understanding of the world.

Each frequency is like speaking a different language. I do not understand Spanish because I have not been taught it. If something is spoken to me in that language, I can't hear the message. But, if someone speaks to me in English, I can make sense of them and understand. The same message, created in many different variations and vibrations, will be shared over and over so it can be received clearly by as many people as possible. If you have picked up this book and felt your energy resonating with it, your energy is aligned to the same frequency.

Even while writing this book my frequency level has continued to enhance as I practice, composting my own ego and aligning with my highest self. Those who are not on the same frequency level as the words being written in this book may not hear the message the same and that is okay. Each of us has our own unique journey. The same message may come from another source, and it will click, or maybe even in re-reading the message in this book, you will feel it from a different energy and understand it from a different level of comprehension.

This reminds me of the verses in the Bible about spreading seeds and how some will take root and others will not. Each seed goes through their own individual process of dying and shedding the outer shell in order to grow. Once the seed's shell is disposed of, it dies to this part of itself, and the embryo inside takes root, growing into the plant it holds within. It must also have the right energies around it to do so, the right temperature, hydration, and soil. In the right environment, the plant can flourish and grow into its full abundance. Just like a seed, the human ego must also die to parts of itself to grow. Dying to self, being reborn, and developing a connection to the true self, allows us to grow in abundance as well.

The Parable of the Sower:

"Behold, a farmer went out to sow. As he sowed, some seeds fell by the roadside, and the birds came and devoured them. Others fell on rocky ground, where they didn't have much soil, and immediately they sprang up, because they had no depth of earth. When the sun had risen, they were scorched. Because they had no root, they withered away. Others fell among thorns. The thorns grew up and choked them. Others fell on good soil and yielded fruit: some one hundred times as much, some sixty, and

some thirty. He who has ears to

hear, let him hear."

or thirty times what was sown.

Whoever has ears, let them hear."

The World English Bible; Matthew 13:1-23

As Jesus said, *whoever has ears to hear, let them hear.*

Think about this for a moment; spend some time meditating on it: Every single thing ever created on this planet, every object we can hold, every tangible item, every product and service, all came from a single thought that expanded into a greater energy. This is the energy of manifestation in the physical. That is why even in the Bible it says that "God spoke, and it was created." To speak, it must first be a thought, and thoughts create energy. We are energy. So instead of finding yourself in competition with others who may be sharing or doing something similar, or rejecting a message because you've heard it before, allow your ego to step back and understand that the same message takes many forms to reach many types of people, and even to reach you as many times as needed for you to be able to make the most use of it.

You can read something 99 times, and suddenly after the hundredth, it finally clicks. Growth requires repetition, continual practice, returning over and over to what you are learning, dying to the old self, putting in the energy and practice to align with your spirit. Slowly you will be releasing the ego's fear, the need to stay small or hidden, and allowing your energy to change by hearing once again the same message, so you can begin attracting something new into your life.

You are attracted to vibrations and frequencies that resonate with your own, and the same is attracted to you. Once you understand this principle, you will know how to work on yourself to develop a deeper connection to your highest potential. Without these insights, we remain in the cycle of repeating the same experiences over and over in our lives because we never address the underlying energetics of our circumstance.

None of us is ever truly alone—we are always connected to the energy of the universe, and to one to another. To truly compost the ego, we must continue to bring our awareness back to this place. As you find yourself at the end of this book and possibly looking for ways to implement the teachings you have read, remember love is the most important energy you can hold, especially towards yourself. It is not selfish or wrong to put yourself first. Allowing yourself to have moments of putting yourself first and practicing the silencing of your mind will strengthen your connection with your highest self, which enhances the connections around you. It is also not wrong to disconnect from the world completely at times to realign with your highest self. Guilt or shame may arise to dissuade you in these moments, but shame is only the ego's response to releasing the old energies it has held. Healing parts of the ego that no longer serve us requires a continual dying to self, but even more self-compassion and love.

Our paths are not meant to be straight. We will mess up, make mistakes, and take wrong turns. But we must remind ourselves that this is the reason we are living as humans in the first place. Over time you will gain more tools to implement the changes you want in your life. Try not to worry about how quickly it happens, or even how it will happen. The universe has a way of bringing things to us when we are ready. That is the work of the spirit self, not ego. When we release the need to control, we move forward. Even if there are areas in your life your spirit continually takes you back to in attempts to heal, each time you allow the process to happen, you become more and more in alignment with your highest self, letting go of what holds you back little by little.

As you let go, you open up the ability to see how you can truly manifest good in your life without holding on to things that no longer serve you. Once you understand how energy is flowing through you, in you, and around you, you'll know what to release and how to do so. Beliefs, thoughts, behaviors, fears…all of these are direct reflections of the energy you hold in you. None of the energy you hold in you is wrong, it is just where you are at the moment, and that is okay. Accepting this place in peace and trusting the healing process to move you forward will help you relax enough to dive into the process of composting parts of the ego again and again.

Composting the ego, rewiring it, and creating new understandings within it, will allow it to release its hold on your life, develop a new frequency, and calm enough to allow your spirit to be seen. Pain is our teacher and discomfort our diving board. Each event, each relationship, each trauma, each energy exchange in your life brought you to the place you are right now. You have the ability to manifest the life you are meant to live in this lifetime. You are a marvelous being, with much potential, whether you believe it at this moment or not. Each person is made directly from the original source of all things. The air we breathe, the voice we speak, the eyes we see out of, the heart and brain that keep our bodies alive, all of it is a direct reflection of the I Am. You are the universe's energy, and the universe's energy is you. It truly is a remarkable thing to have this power and energy within, and the ability to align with it. As you continue the cycle of composting the ego, connecting back within your spirit, I hope you find peace and learn to trust that you really can lay back like a leaf in a stream, letting it carry you exactly where you are meant to be in this life. You just have to release, let go, and trust the flow.

A drawing of guides when they first presented themselves to Angie.

References:
Leaf Lessons; When Trauma and Religion Collide the Process of Spiritual Awakening and Healing.
Rider Waite Tarot
The Story of Two Wolfs – Unknown Original Origin
https://www.worldometers.info/world-population/
The World English Bible
https://ebible.org/web/copyright.htm
The World English Bible (WEB) is a Public Domain (no copyright) Modern English translation of the Holy Bible. That means that you may freely copy it in any form, including electronic and print formats. The World English Bible is based on the American Standard Version of the Holy Bible first published in 1901, the Biblia Hebraica Stutgartensa Old Testament, and the Greek Majority Text New Testament. It is in draft form, and currently being edited for accuracy and readability.

About the Author

Angie Harris has over 18 years of experience working with clients, supporting them, and guiding them on their personal journey of healing. Gifted with Intuitive insights and ability to read energy, she provides tools and guidance in reconnecting people with their highest self. Her books are written through intuitive insight from personal experiences and deep connection with spirit.

Angie is the CEO of Leaf Lessons, and created the Women Awakened Healing Circle which she meets monthly with a group of women providing support and guidance. She also holds healing workshops, and provides one-on-one intuitive healing support for clients all around the world. Gifted in mediumship and ability to read energy she helps reconnect clients back with their true self, releasing barriers keeping them stuck in unwanted cycles in their lives.

Angie is certified in Meditation & Mindfulness, Sound Healing Therapy, and is a Usui Reiki Master. She also received her AA. in Biblical Studies, and BAS in Human Services with emphasis in Victim Survivor Services and focus on Trauma Based Approaches.
To reach Angie visit; www.leaflessons.org